GW00691185

Change in a Changing World

The Golden Blade 1993

Anthroposophy springs from the work and teaching of
Rudolf Steiner (1861–1925). He describes it as a "path
of knowledge, to guide the spiritual in the human being
to the spiritual in the universe."

The aim of this annual is to bring the outlook of
anthroposophy to bear on questions and activities of
evident relevance to the present, in a way which may
have a lasting value. It was founded in 1949 by Charles
Davy and Arnold Freeman, who were its first editors.

The title derives from an old Persian legend,
according to which King Djemjdid received from his
god, Ahura Mazdao, a golden blade with which to fulfil
his mission on earth. It carried the heavenly forces of
light into the darkness of earthly substance, thus
allowing its transformation. The legend points to the
possibility that man, through wise and compassionate
work with the earth, can one day regain on a new level
what was lost when the Age of Gold was supplanted by
those of Silver, Bronze and Iron. Technology could
serve this aim; instead of endangering our planet's life,
it could help to make the earth a new sun.

Change
in a Changing World

The Golden Blade No.45

Edited by William Forward
and Andrew Wolpert

Floris Books

First published in English in 1992 by Floris Books.

© 1992 Floris Books, Edinburgh
All rights reserved. No part of this publication may
be reproduced without the prior permission of
Floris Books, 15 Harrison Gardens, Edinburgh.

British Library CIP Data available

ISBN 0-86315-150-7
ISSN 0967-6708

Printed in Great Britain
by BPCC Wheatons Ltd, Exeter

I pass through the pores of the ocean and shores;
I change, but I cannot die

Shelley (1792–1822)

In books and love, the mind one end pursues
And only change the expiring flame renews

John Gay (1685–1732)

For all that moveth doth in change delight

Spencer (1522–99)

Behold, I show you a mystery; we shall not all sleep,
but we shall all be changed, in a moment, in the
twinkling of an eye, at the last trump: for the trumpet
shall sound, and the dead shall be raised incorruptible,
and we shall be changed.

1 Corinthians 15:51f

Contents

Editorial notes   9

Celebrating Columbus *Paul Law*   11

Upheaval in Adolescence *William Forward*   19

Centring the Teacher *Dorit Winter*   32

Mystery Play is Now *an interview with*
        Christopher Marcus   39

Regenerative Grammar *Andrew Wolpert*   50

Losing Ground *Ria Freiermuth*   58

Finding One's Place *Stephen Briault*   61

The Flowering of the Human Soul in Florence
        Charles Lawrie   72

Review   84

Letter   88

Notes about the authors   91

Editorial notes

"When Gregor Samson woke up one morning from unsettling dreams, he found himself changed in his bed into a monstrous vermin." With these memorable words Franz Kafka opens his disturbing novel *The Metamorphosis* in which a travelling salesman find his life and that of the other members of his family thrown into confusion by this totally unexpected and shattering change. Impossible to understand, it must seem equally impossible to come to terms with and yet, each in their way and only by dint of a change in themselves, each of the characters does so.

Gregor's first reactions have a poignant humour. "What has happened to me?" he thought. It was no dream. His room ... lay quiet between the familiar four walls ... "How about going back to sleep for a few minutes and forgetting all about this nonsense," he thought, but that was completely impracticable ...

For much of the first part of the story Kafka exploits a rich seam of bittersweet humour in the juxtaposition of ordinary everyday thoughts with a totally bizarre situation. Yet this comedy is by no means an end in itself. As W H Auden put it: "Kafka is important to us because his predicament is the predicament of modern man." Any one who has felt totally misunderstood or indeed totally unable to understand a radical change in his relationship to himself and to others will find in this novel much that speaks to him.

In the last few years of this century the pace of change, both inner and outer, is perhaps faster than ever before. The consoling familiar framework of individual and social life is dissolving fast. Not only that, changes are sudden and unpredictable as well as radical.

In this issue of the *Golden Blade* we show from a variety of points of view how the challenge of change is confronted: the writer celebrating Columbus; the teacher meeting the unique demands of unique children; the adolescent in the throes of tumultuous transition and the encounter with evil as an agent of change; the office worker in an environment changing beyond recognition, an individual experience and a more general study; the theatre director on a radical new approach to Rudolf Steiner's mystery plays, the writer drawing parallels with that other great era of change, the Renaissance; and some thoughts on how language itself after such upheaval, whether individual or social, reflects a quest for new meaning. One might say that the whole issue echoes in a variety of ways the puzzled words of Gregor Samson, "What has happened to me?" and points to how the challenge of change can also be the challenge to find meaning.

We would like to express our thanks to the contributors, and also to Imprint Publicity Services who have for some years been our printers and distributors.

We welcome our new association with Floris Books, and are confident that it will enhance the quality that readers of the *Golden Blade* have come to expect.

W.F.
A.W.

Celebrating Columbus

Paul Law

And new Philosophy calls all in doubt,
The Element of fire is quite put out;
The Sun is lost, and th'earth, and no man's wit
Can well direct him where to look for it.
And freely men confesse that this world's spent
When in the Planets, and the Firmament
They seeke so many new: then see that this
Is crumbled out againe to his Atomies.
'Tis all in peeces, all cohearance gone;
All just supply, and all Relation:
Prince, Subject, Father, Sonne, are things forget ...
                    (John Donne: *An Anatomie of the World*)

The "new Philosophy" that John Donne was lamenting so histrionically in 1611 was not really so very new at all; it embraced the comprehensive readjustment of western thinking that had begun with the publication of Copernicus' *On the Revolutions of the Heavenly Spheres* in 1543, and even earlier with Columbus' first voyage to America. Scientific theory and practical exploration produced results that — according to a phrase that was popular at the time — "turned the world upside down." It began with a change in people's picture of the physical cosmos, but it rapidly undermined the most fundamental assumptions that had given coherence to Christian society: within a century man had been dethroned from his special place in creation; the authority of the Church had been replaced by a personal ethics; the popular image of the "commonweal" as a stable and ordained organism had been usurped by the forces of a dynamic and chaotic primitive capitalism. In short, changes became the norm for society, rather than the exception.

But when we survey the centuries that followed, we are likely to think of them as a relatively slow–moving, stable period. And this is the case despite the fact that a very large proportion of what we study as "history" consists of various forms of protest against change. What are these changes, then, that our ancestors protested or applauded, and that we assume ourselves to be subject to in a far higher degree than they? Clearly, we use "change" to describe two things that are closely related yet also distinguishable. Firstly, we have the changes that happen in our technology, our legal, economic, or social status etc., and which oblige us to change ourselves in order to be able to live with them. Secondly, there are the changes in the way we think of ourselves, which come as a consequence of the adjustments we have to make. The first kind of change requires the breaking of habits, a learning of new patterns of behaviour: the second kind of change requires a revision of the picture we have of ourselves and of our habits of thought. Eventually, the second kind of change demands that we revise our picture of our society and its history.

In practice this process of revision can take very different forms. The pressure for change is usually gradual and accumulative, and the individual meets it with many minor adjustments that are too small to be noticeable: this aspect of change is a largely unconscious process. (Think, for example, of the numerous applications of electronics that you have absorbed in the last decade: cumulatively, they have quite likely transformed your style of living and working; they have also subtly altered the way you think of personal relationships, money, time, travel, global, politics, human evolution, medicine ... yet for most people, the scale of changes and significance of the changes will only become apparent in retrospect.)

Under other circumstances the pressure for change induces a cumulative pressure of resistance: people accept change at one level — because they have no choice — but they reject it at another level. The build-up of pressure resembles the tension that grows at the junction of continental plates: and the resulting earthquake has its counterpart in social revolution. The popular concept of revolution highlights its forward-looking or progressive tendency, but the *motor* of revolution is frequently a demand to return to an earlier condition. The two most violent revolutions of the century — the Russian revolutions of 1917 and the Nazi seizure of power in 1933 — both had overwhelmingly reactionary undercurrents. In Russia, the appeal to *Vohd,* (the autocratic rule of the "little father," the Tsar) to restore the justice and stability of the traditional society found its fulfilment in the domination of the ultimate autocrat, Stalin. In Germany, the rejection of a dynamic but unstable capitalism produced bizarre Nazi ideology in which German men, having conquered the world by their mastery of technological warfare, would return to the soil as peasant farmers; craftsmen would be organized in medieval guilds; women would busy themselves with baking and childbearing; and society would be ruled by an elite of Arthurian knights. Both ideologies — Marxism and Nazism — recognized the key importance of rewriting history in order to harness the forces of revolution: they appealed so strongly because they offered a vision of the future which, as it was essentially drawn from the past, had the enchantment of certainty.

The examples I have taken were both cases in which societies turned to history as a means of coping with painful and unwanted forces of changes. The fact that Soviet Russia and Nazi Germany used versions of history to manipulate their population into submitting to an ideology should not lead us to reject the teaching of history altogether: one of the primary uses of history is to help us adjust to the present by revising our picture of the past. This does not mean that we falsify the past: it means that we reinterpret it from our new perspective and use it to make sense of the present. We should be aware that history in this modern sense is a recent invention: its emergence and development parallels that of the consciousness soul. Because the subject matter of history is so bound up with the past, we are likely to think of history itself as an ancient activity — we are likely to confuse it with the preservation of continuity with the past that was the major intellectual and artistic activity of pre-renaissance society. But history proper — perhaps we should call it critical history in order to distinguish it from monumental history — only becomes necessary when the past is under threat, when society becomes dynamic and fragmented, and when individual consciousness becomes actively engaged in the creation of a personal perspective on human destiny.This creation is a painful process, like any other process of birth, and it is man's efforts to escape this pain that have given rise to the themes of class, nation, and race in modern history — the desperate search for a group soul in which incipient selfhood can be immersed.

If we perceive history as a process of revision in response to forces of change, we shall also perceive the practice of historical thinking as intimately bound up with individual freedom. To think historically is to be able to define and modify one's self-image in a profound sense: to be deprived of historical skills, or to fall victim to historical propaganda, is to be imprisoned — to be spiritually unfree. A society's attitude to the teaching of historical skills is consequently an important symptom of its social conditions, perhaps even of its general spiritual health.

It is instructive in this regard to examine the changing attitudes to history teaching in contemporary western society. In my own childhood (1950s) the teaching of history in English schools was still complacently Anglo-centric. The Commonwealth had replaced the Empire, the sun had finally set on the Raj, but the Englishman's view of his nation's past as an unfaltering procession of moral and technological triumphs remained unshaken. It had largely been Englishmen, after all, who had discovered the rest of the world and who had brought it civilization (by which an Englishmen mostly means plumbing), missionaries, and sensible democratic institutions. Fellow white men in Europe and the colonies had their minor share of recognition in the great work.

By the time that I returned to schools to teach in them, the perspectives were rapidly changing, and they have been in a state of turmoil since. People began to notice that Britain was a pluralist society, a melange of various ethnic, cultural and religious streams; and that beyond the shores of the island fortress was a global economy, a global society. To live and work in this world meant that a wide range of deep-seated attitudes and assumptions would have to be dropped.

In the 1970s the history curriculum was transformed. British schools discovered Europe; and as a kind of after-thought, the World. More importantly, the history of colonial-ism began to be taught from the perspective of third world peoples; and the American Indians, who had only previously appeared as extras in Hollywood westerns, suddenly made a come-back as peace-loving ecologists. The problem with wholesale revision of this kind was that it had implications beyond the classroom or lecture-hall; the more so as it was accompanied by a new militancy in various ethnic groups within the country. The demands of Islamic communities in Bradford to have their children taught in Arabic, or for Sikh boys in Manchester to retain their turbans during games lesson, provoked a cultural backlash that quickly found political expression. Harmless history teachers were henceforth seen as a group of sinister bearded academics with loony-left sympathies. The teaching of history appeared to be a subvers-ive activity.

One answer was to abolish history. This was achieved in the late 1980's by the introduction of a new history curriculum which effectively limited historical studies to the interpretation of documents. What is history for? asked the Department of

Education. History is for the acquisition of those skills which
the study of history practises, came the answer. Henceforth,
the study of history was justified because it taught you how to
interpret documents, sift information, and evaluate evidence —
all skills with a strong economic value.

By limiting history to the interpretation of documents, the
scope of history itself was limited to the period of the indus-
trial revolution and beyond; and for the overwhelming major-
ity of students this is where history henceforth began: in
Victorian England or the twentieth century — i.e. a period
whose fundamental conditions are identical with the present,
and which consequently offers very little measure of the
present. Underlying this development is the invasion of the
spiritual life (of which the study of history is a vital part) by
the forces of the economic life. Economic forces strive to
abolish historicism, just as they strive to establish utilitarian-
ism: for a society without roots, without cultural or class
loyalties, is economically mobile in a way that a historically
conscious society can never be.

The most recent developments in the history curriculum
reveal the continuing uncertainty of our response to the forces
of change. The newly published National Curriculum is a
straightforward attempt to put the clock back: henceforth there
will be a return to national history, with more dates, more
battles, more great lives. The emphasis will be on "national
heritage" and achievement: the perspective will be Anglo– and
Euro– and Christo–centric — John of Gaunt with a touch of
Erasmus.

This all brings us to 1992 and the five hundredth anniversary of Columbus' voyage to America. And it raises the
dreadful question: to celebrate or not to celebrate? The
question has unleashed a public debate on both sides of the
Atlantic, and it highlights the polarization of views as to how
our society should reconcile its past to the forces of change
that face it.

The "traditionalists" see Columbus as a key figure in the

march of progress, the expansion of the West, the foundation of modern America. The "revisionists" see him as a perpetrator of genocide, a looter, and a chauvinist pirate. For one party, to neglect the anniversary would amount to a betrayal of national and cultural identity: for the other party, a celebration would be a gross cultural insult, a perpetuation of white racial dominance.

I did not discover the strength of feeling behind the issue till I began work on a children's opera to celebrate Columbus' voyage. The opera was to have been performed in a number of London schools with a mixed race population. Early in the planning stage, teachers in the schools began to raise objections. For many of their pupils, they explained, Columbus was an emblem of white superiority. Far form celebrating Columbus, he was best forgotten altogether: he was a hysterical unperson. If anything should be taught about Columbus, it was the story of his victims — or the victims of the white invasion that he made possible: it was the story of the extermination of the Indian tribes, the looting of the Meso–American empires, the establishment of negro slavery, the continued white exploitation of the third world peoples.

The more I discussed the question with people, the more I became aware of a kind of cultural impasse. You were expected to take sides; yet it was a conflict that by its nature did not offer the hope of resolution. Our pluralist society was demanding that we revise our picture of the past, that we come to a new understanding of each other; but the reaction of both sides was to polemize the past and to polarize the issues which it raised.

Instead of abandoning the opera, I began to perceive its purpose in a different light: it had to address the question of reconciliation — it had to present the historical event in such a way that it would assist both sides of the debate in coming to terms with it and in coming closer to each other. As work proceeded I began to see that Columbus' landing in America as a tragic parallel to the divisions of our own society: Two groups of people from different cultural backgrounds encounter each other: they are aware of the enormous potential for good that lies in that meeting, but they are also beset by fears, limitations, personal weakness. There is an underlying willingness to learn, but a danger that one side will assume superiority. I wrote the opera from the perspective of the native Indian population and from the more intuitive consciousness that they possessed, and I struggled to dispel the dangerous illusion that there are passive victims in the course of human evolution. The suffering of the native peoples of America and of the negro slaves who followed them was the result of crime, but it was also a sacrifice: both sides in the encounter have made their contribution to the creation of the present.

I began to see that the anniversary of Columbus' voyage was of far greater importance than its place in the "monumental" history of the West. If history creates occasion for polarization or vengeance, it also gives the opportunity for forgiveness. To think of oneself as a victim, or to regret the past actions of one's own race or society is of little consequence in human evolution. What matters is our ability to forgive and to accept forgiveness, to resolve that the future will not repeat the mistakes of the past. It is time we changed our views of the events of 1492 — all of us.

Upheaval in Adolescence

Finding meaning in the encounter with evil

W.B. Forward

Rescued from the flames of the burning of the first Goetheanum and housed now in the eloquent concrete of the second
is Rudolf Steiner's powerful sculpture of the *Representative of
Man.* It is a group of figures in wood showing the Human
Being as in the midst of Evil, surrounded as it were.

What distinguishes the human figure from the others is the
quality of uprightness, reminiscent of the advice of Christ in
the St. Luke apocalypse: "When all this begins to happen,
stand upright and hold your heads high, because your libera-
tion is near." The picture is one of an ego being, holding the
balance, exercising judgment. This capacity is however only
fully present in us normally when we have reached the age of
full adulthood, around 21. Until then it is the task of those
around us to exercise it on our behalf to a greater or lesser
extent. For the first two seven-year phases of growing up this
is relatively unproblematic but in the third it is anything but
so. Yet it is precisely in the period of adolescence that the
young person seems to be subjected to trials as an individual.
In many cultures this entry into a period of trials is marked
with a ceremony that had something of the character of an
initiation, and even where it is not, the young person will
often seek an experience which says to him or her, "remember
the importance of this moment in your life." From then on the
bringing to birth of this ego is a struggle, and is by no means

assured of a successful outcome. It becomes apparent in each
biography that the question of freedom is inextricably linked
with the encounter with evil. As the pace of change and social
upheaval has increased in this century, it is perhaps no
accident that adolescent issues have come into the foreground
as they have.

But what exactly is evil? Tackled purely with the intellect
the question generally produces unsatisfactory answers, often
indeed a denial that evil as such exists. Much more can be
gained from contemplating the archetypal pictures in which it
has been represented artistically. Pupils in the Waldorf schools
are fortunate to have such pictures brought to them annually
in the form of the Oberufer Christmas plays — though perhaps
they don't always see it that way themselves! In both the
Paradise play and the Kings play one finds archetypal encounters with evil and its consequences both of which are echoed
in each individual's biography during the adolescent years.

With the Paradise play it is the Fall. In picture form we see
the intellectual awakening and the descent into matter (physical growth spurt and sexual maturity) which are characteristic
of puberty. There is deep wisdom in such pictures. The
vertebrae enclose a hollow space, separating off as it were
from the rest of the world, and joined together in a spinal
column form the basis for the experience of egoity. The snake
in its build shows a predominance of vertebrae and even in the
context of biological evolution echoes the coming out of the
paradisal watery element onto the earth. Its capacity to coil up
on itself emphasizes the aspect of self–centredness that
accompanies the temptation "Like to a God thou canst become." With the eating of the apple of premature knowledge,
Adam utters what is the experience of every adolescent: "Ah,
how my soul is overthrown!" The consequences follow on —
expulsion: the last vestiges of the dreamy consciousness of
childhood are shed; exposure: on the one hand a sensitivity to
that new element in the young person which has yet to be
recognized, on the other the feeling that the scenes of child-

hood are now bare, stripped of their magic; opened eyes: open indeed to the world of the senses but closed to the world of which Wordsworth and Thomas Traherne speak in *Intimations* and *Dumnesse*; pain: many things which previously were easy now suddenly become difficult, painting & music, movement and maths but also communication even with loved ones; labour: there is a tremendous release of energy in this phase and a corresponding increase in the capacity for work; disease: very often there is in addition to the many ailments of adolescence a sense of dis-ease in the rapidly growing physical body; death: it can be experienced how taxing the nervous system has this effect on the physical body; the curse to humanity extending to the earth as a whole; rarely can this have been more readily experienced by the young person than now. Yet there is also a promising, positive outcome: to the fallen Satan God says, "See now, this Adam such wealth has won. Like to a God he is become. Knowledge he has of evil and good. He can lift up his hand on high, whereby he liveth eternally." The capacity to lift up is there which holds the promise of humanity finding its way back to the source of life. There is the possibility of directing these new-found powers to the good.

In the Shepherds play, which is shown to all ages, this hope is confirmed by the voluntary descent into earthly conditions of the God of Love, who did not fall into them — a second great act of sacrifice after the creation. Then in the third of the trilogy which is shown only to adolescents and those just coming into adolescence we find a picture of how to come to terms with the challenge of this phase. Rudolf Steiner speaks of how at the birth of the astral, feeling body there is a more or less unconscious perception of one's pre-earthly intentions and origins which, even if only unconsciously perceived, can account for the teenager's difficulties in accepting the world as he finds it. There remains however a powerful yearning towards the ideal which if it is rightly met will bring the young person on course into a fruitful adulthood. The picture of the kings seeing the star, following it to wherever it might lead, going astray, finding each other and only then rediscovering it, is a powerfully nourishing one for the adolescent. The red king who stands at the moment of choice with the fraught question: "Here are two ways, which is the right?" speaks for those who watch, and the appearance of the star holds out hope of finding the right one. The reverse is true of Herod who clinging to the false security of earthly power is manipulated by the devil into multiplying evil all around him.

How can we better understand this experience of the Fall? In *Soul Economy and Waldorf Education*,* Rudolf Steiner puts it like this:

> What is it that the adolescent brings with him when he "breaks through" into the external world via his bony system? It is what originally he had brought down with him from pre–earthly existence and what, gradually had become interwoven with his whole inner being. And now, with the onset of sexual maturity, the adolescent is being cast out of the spiritual world, as it were. Without exaggerating, one can really put it that strongly, for it represents the actual truth; with the coming of puberty the young human being is cast out from the living world of the spirit, and thrown into the external world which he or she can perceive only by means of the physical and etheric body. And though the adolescent is not at all aware of what is going on inside him, subconsciously this plays an all the more intense part. Sub-consciously or semi–consciously, it makes the adolescent compare the world he has now entered with the world which he formerly had within himself. Previously, he had not experienced the spiritual world consciously but, nevertheless, he had found it possible to live in harmony with it. His inner being

---

* Lecture 13, page 227, Anthroposophic Press 1986.

felt attuned to it and ready to co-operate freely with
the soul and spiritual realm. But now, in these
changed conditions, the external world no longer
offers such possibilities to him. It presents all kinds
of hindrances which, in themselves, create the wish to
overcome them. This in turn, gives rise to the
tumultuous relationship between the adolescent and
the surrounding world, lasting from the fourteenth or
fifteenth year till the beginning of the twenties.

On the one hand then, a kind of loss, but on the other a
momentous gain, for maturing in the womb of the child's
social environment the astral body which emerges at puberty
reveals a new capacity:

... there rises up in him a new feeling, an entirely
new appraisal of mankind as a whole. It is this new
experience of humankind which represents the
spiritual counterpart to the physical faculty of
reproduction. Physically he becomes able to
procreate. Spiritually, he becomes capable of
experiencing mankind as a totality.*

Seen in the context, not so much of the individual biography (though the parallels are evident) as of the evolution of
the human race, the phenomenon of male and female sexuality
is described by Rudolf Steiner in his lectures on the Akashic
Record as a consequence of the densification of earthly matter
to the point where the human being is no longer able to reproduce itself without help from another, opposite faculty of
reproduction. In consequence part of the individual's reproduc-
tive power is released, i.e. not employed in this way.

This power is directed inwards in the human being. It
cannot work outwardly and so becomes available for
the development of inner organs. This then is an
important moment in the development of mankind.
Previously what we call the spirit, the capacity for

* *Idem*, page 232.

thinking, was unable to find its place in the human
being. For this capacity would not have found an
organ enabling it to function. The soul had directed
all its powers outwards, to build up the human body.
But now the power of the soul which is not employed
outwardly is able to enter into relation with the power
of the spirit and as a result of this, organs are
developed in the body which later on enable the
human being to become a thinking being. Thus man
was able to use a part of the strength which was
formerly employed in reproducing himself for the
purpose of perfecting his own being. The power by
means of which humanity develops for itself a
thinking brain is the same by means of which each
individual fructified itself in former times. Thinking
came about through the division of the sexes. ... The
soul has both male and female qualities. In former
times it fashioned its body in the same way. Later it
was only able to form it so that it had to co-operate
with another body in order to reproduce; the soul
itself thereby acquired the capacity to work with the
spirit. Outwardly the soul is fructified from without,
inwardly it is fructified from within, by the spirit.*

Here then we find again the two qualities of the kings in the
Oberufer play: the power to ennoble the self so that the
meaning of the star can be perceived and become a guide in
life and secondly the power to reach out and find in others
representatives of humanity as a whole.

How now has this astral, starry body whose birth takes
place at puberty worked in the young human being before this
moment? In the first seven-year phase of the child's life we
know from Rudolf Steiner's research that much of the human
being's inner energy is directed towards building up its physi-

---

* *Aus der Akasha Chronik*, p. 75ff (translated as *Cosmic Memory*, Rudolf
Steiner Publications, Inc. 1959.)

cal organs from the warp and weft of sense impressions of each day. In this period the function of this astral intelligence is to ward off the impact of the future and allow the creative forces of the past working from the head down to work at weaving sense impressions into the physical organism. Strong awakening impulses from without or emotional scenes will often result in a physical reaction in the form of an illness.

In the second phase from seven to fourteen this is metamorphosed into a defence against what comes from within the organism now that the child is looking in increasingly aware wonder at the world around it. The tendency of sense impressions to send one to sleep is resisted as the reaction in sympathy or antipathy gains in importance. One can often observe in children of this age a certain disgust for the processes of the physical body, towards the middle of the period a heightened sensitivity to physical deformity of any kind, a "Yuk!" reaction to a tummy rumble, a sneeze, a wart or a mole. Compared with the first phase there is now a breathing in of the world following a breathing out of the cosmos and the activity of intelligence is largely to hold back the workings of the past, the inside bodily processes.

By analogy one could say that the first period is devoted to the building of the instrument, the second to allowing the world to sound through it as the sympathies and antipathies respond. This gradual emergence of the personality in response to its surroundings is also suggested by the Latin origin of the word — *per sonare* — to sound through. As the child experiences this hollow resounding space of its instrument there can come the early experiences of its own individuality, experiences often of loneliness, the more acute since the power to express this individuality is not yet there. Impressions and their feeling response thus do not get *ex*pressed but rather *im*pressed on the memory body which is particularly strongly developed at this time. This is the dominant mood of this seven–to–fourteen–year period: wonder — taking in, being consciously impressed but not yet able to produce a corresponding individual expression, response. All the time it is being kept in check somewhat by the element of disgust. This latter delays the birth of the astral body while wonder tends to accelerate it.

With the birth of the astral body at around fourteen a further metamorphosis tales place. The mood of wonder is replaced by one of fear as the connection with the world of the spirit fades and the awareness is increasingly there, that here is a being which makes its own impact on the world which is beginning to have a certain responsibility. With it comes also a powerful surge of energy and the will to reach out and make contact with others.

Together with the disgust of the previous period this subtle fear or experience of nakedness of the soul produces a new feeling which is a keynote of the third period (fourteen to twenty-one), namely that of shame, shame in the sense of a feeling of inadequacy in the face of the challenge of the future but also of a momentary loss of the ideal self-image recalled however dimly from one's pre-birth intentions.

This feeling of shame arises when the fear is stronger than the disgust. If the reverse is true and the disgust dominates, then another feeling peculiar to this period emerges, namely that of doubt. These may not seem very positive attributes to be starting out with on a new phase of development but it should be remembered that doubt makes possible critical thinking in which the ego, which is now coming to birth, can increasingly experience itself. Shame on the other hand can lead to an ennobling of the powerful forces of desire, a taking in hand of one's own moral development which again is a way in which the gradually emerging ego can make itself felt. The newly born astral body thus becomes an organ of expression for the ego. The instrument which has been built and has developed its own peculiar resonance can to played upon, as Karl König put it, the individuality "begins to speak of itself, to utter its name, to describe its own being."

In this momentous meeting of the inner with the outer the heart as a balancing organ comes into its own, finding the measure of this and all the other polarities experienced so strongly now by the young person. The loneliness that comes of doubt and the yearning that comes of shame find their expression in the powerful beat of the adolescent heart. Being torn between the demands of eros on the one hand and ideal-ism on the other one can experience acutely the forming of a middle ground where a sense of justice, of compassion and of moral values takes shape for the individual. Out of eros can be fashioned courage, for that is what the true meeting of and commitment to the other takes. Out of idealism, faithfulness or a sense of responsibility for these are of more lasting value than any individual achievement can be in the pursuit of an ideal. Out of the sense of justice the imagination to meet the requirements of each individual situation. Socially these virtues demand their counterparts in the recognition of the freedom of the other, the perception, despite all distinctions, of our equality as human beings and the acceptance of responsibility for each other in brotherhood.

One of the ways in which these developments in the adolescent are nourished in the Waldorf schools is through a study of the Parzival legend in which, in archetypal form, many of the key moments of adolescence are represented.

The young Parzival is depicted as feeling a tightness in the breast in response to the song of the birds. The mother becomes anxious as she recognizes the symptoms and in the resulting conversation Parzival asks: "Oh mother, what is God?" The picture he is given is: "... He who took on a shape in the likeness of Man is brighter than the sun ... steadfast love ... Then there is one called Lord of Hell. He is black, perfidy cleaves to him. Turn your thoughts away from him and treacherous despair." Parzival has led a sheltered childhood in a remote forest and when he then for the first time sees a knight with armour glistening in the sunlight he immediately thinks of God. Far from finding God, however, he has found his task in life and the people he wishes to emulate. "Mother, I saw four knights, brighter even than God — they told me about knighthood. Arthur's kingly power must guide me to knightly honour and the office of the Shield!" It is in pursuit of these that he will come to know in a conscious way both God and the devil.

With the best intentions, that is, following the advice his mother gave him to the letter, he enters into adult life leaving behind him a trail of destruction. He does not notice how, as he leaves, his mother dies of heartbreak. His encounter with the beautiful Jeschute alone in her tent is also well intentioned but leaves her to suffer terrible consequences at the hands of her jealous husband. Sigune, whom he now meets has just lost her lover Schionatulander who was killed in defence of Parzival's territories. With the knowledge he gains from her of his earthly responsibilities comes also his name Parzival and its meaning (straight through or pierce through the heart). The first conscious link is made with his own destiny. As he moves to take his place in society — at the table of King Arthur — he takes by force the red armour and horse of Ither, a rebel who stands outside the court challenging it. He then becomes the red knight himself but, again unwittingly, takes on the destiny mantle of Cain — for he has slain his own kinsman. Even the beautiful Cunneware, the first to recognize Parzival's high calling, must suffer blows for it. This at least Parzival is aware of, and he vows to avenge her. From the old knight Gurnemanz Parzival then learns how to take his place as a knight in the world of his time. His conventional education, for such it is, keeps him in touch with the spiritual-ity of the past: "Never lose your sense of shame," but tragically cuts him off from the spirituality of the future: "Do not ask many questions."

When Parzival then comes unknowing to the great challenge of his life, to lift the spell on the Grail Castle, he does not have the power to become knowing, to ask the question. He leaves the castle still unknowing. Whilst he soon begins to put

right some of the wrongs he has perceived (reuniting Jeschute
and Orilus, restoring the honour of Cunneware) and rapidly
gains credit for this outer success, it is not until he has reached
the peak of this outer success, with King Arthur and his court
coming to seek him out that he is confronted with the full
import of his inner failure. The meeting with Cundrie leaves
him with a deep sense of shame. Not only that, his faith in
God is shaken. When Gawain wishes him godspeed he replies:
"Alas, what is God? Were He all powerful, He would not have
brought us to such shame." He goes on his quest accompanied
by both shame and doubt.

After years in the wilderness, he is moved by the humility
of pilgrims on Good Friday to accept that he also has sinned,
erred, gone astray, and seeks counsel. In the long conversation
with Trevrizent he gets to see himself in the context of the
development of humanity in the cosmos, of the Grail family
(of which he is a member) and of his own biography (he
learns for the first time of his mother's fate and his relationship to Ither). In each of these he can now see how evil has
played a role. The Parzival who leaves Trevrizent is a knowing one whose aim is to be found worthy to be a vessel for
something higher than himself. Indeed when he is placed a
second time in a position to ask the question of Amfortas, this
time knowing what he has to do, he prays for grace before
doing so.

Thus the encounter with evil in Parzival's quest is intimately
bound up with his coming to consciousness, knowledge and
ultimately freedom.

The twofold nature of evil — on the one hand the tendency
to pride and on the other to cold, lifeless intellectualism — is
recognized in this great imagination and we thus have two
heroes (or two heroic aspects of the same being) each overcoming one. Parzival overcoming Luciferic pride with humility
and Gawain overcoming the Ahrimanic power of illusion by
calm acceptance and perseverance.

None of the above would be presented in such an interpretative way to pupils, but the images have a vitality that enables young people to recognize their own experience in them.

The upheaval and reorientation of adolescence, the getting-to-know in the encounter with evil, affects the whole human being, body, soul and spirit and has done so for centuries. The ways in which the threats and challenges to humanity manifest, change with the times. To look just at the soul level one can see how the struggle must be to meet (i) a tendency to mechanize the thinking to reduce it to endless permutations of yes/no combinations, none of which relate to an imaginative whole; (ii) a tendency to make shallow and dull or vegetable-like the feelings by for instance random, unrelated juxtaposition of impressions and (iii) a tendency to animalize the will — one notices for instance how people talk of the body now: dispassionately, as if it were just another personal asset or prop. Moreover it is increasingly apparent that these forces of the soul are becoming dissociated one from another — actions can be carried out to which one has no feeling relationship ("I don't know why I did it"), thoughts can develop an inhuman logic of their own.

What than can be done to help? If one sees the adolescent as a kind of tightrope walker struggling to find his balance, then direct outer involvement might do as much harm as good. One can do much as a teacher however by strengthening that balancing capacity in oneself in a way that one leaves the young person free to relate to it or not. Jörgen Smit describes in his book on the meditative deepening of education how the teacher can help to re-establish or maintain the relationship of the pupil with his own spiritual helpers in sleep. Every effort one makes to overcome something in oneself requires the warmth, uprightness and ego strength that was the gift to humanity of the Archai. Every effort made to deepen one's listening and to fill one's speech with warmth and the fire of ideals will strengthen the night-time link of the young people with the Archangels, whose gift to humanity was speech.

Every effort to bring fantasy backed by sound observation into one's thinking will strengthen the pupils link with their angels in sleep whose gift to humanity was thinking.

Trevrizent's response to the plight of Amfortas his brother and Parzival his nephew was not to tell them what they should have done, or should not have done, but rather to take upon himself additional disciplines of the soul and spirit.

A daily look back at the events of the day taking note perhaps not only of what did happen but also of what did not, or was prevented from happening, can create a space in one's experience of the day which allows for gradual perception of the work of the angels in arranging our destiny. In all humility one can thus strive to become a co-worker of these spiritual beings.

The story of Faust which is often brought to the pupils in their last year at school shows the human being in a evolving relationship with the figure of evil: initially manipulated by Mephistopheles, but later increasingly keeping him busy by means of constant striving, until after death Faust, far from being condemned to hell is welcomed into the ranks of the heavenly hierarchies as one who can bring something that was not there before. This is the image of the mature human ego at work in the world, surrounded indeed by evil but undaunted by it.

Centring the Teacher in uncentred times

Dorit Winter

Children grow. They grow and they change. They have their rhythms and their cycles and a measure of regularity attends their growth, With a bit of practice, we recognize the kinder-garten dervish, the equable fifth grader, the graduating senior at sight. If you were to glance through a stack of old year-books looking up fifth graders, you would find that whether they were fifth graders last year or three decades ago there is a certain consistency. Fifth graders look like fifth graders. There is a fifth grade height to their bodies, a fifth grade expression of serio–comic/earthy–dreaminess on their faces. Disregarding styles of hair and clothing, you would find essential similarities between a group of children who are now in fifth grade, and those who were eleven years old thirty years ago. But if you could peel away the paper on which they have been preserved, to enter life as they knew it three decades ago, you would find that a fifth grader's world in the sixties was conspicuously different from a fifth grader's world now. If these two groups of children were to meet, their frames of reference would overlap very little. Some obvious differences come to mind, the foremost being the current ubiquity of the computer and all its by–products in communi-cations, entertainment, and ordinary daily transactions. Politics and the steady erosion of the environment have also altered the sense of planet. "Global consciousness," is a phrase, which, like "IBM compatible" did not "interface" with the average eleven year old of thirty years ago. Nor had sex and violence become such publicly sensationalized attendants.

Yet, in spite of the dizzying instability of outer events, eleven years of human development in 1992 are not so very different from eleven years of development in 1962. Nintendo may have replaced the hula-hoop as the toy of choice, but in the larger scheme of things, the scheme of human evolution, an eleven year old is still entering the last half of his second seven year cycle. His physical and etheric sheaths are already beginning to "release" the astral sheath, allowing it gradually to come into its own. This final phase of etheric development, which precedes the approach of the astral forces carries the child through sixth, seventh and eighth grades. It is called pre-adolescence and is a test for any teacher's determination. Informing this determination is the Waldorf teacher's greatest ally: the curriculum. The curriculum recognizes, understands, and nourishes the pre-adolescent now, as it did thirty years ago, as it did seventy years ago. From within, the child is still proceeding through an orderly process of incarnation, while from without he is exposed to those same fracturing influences which have favoured cultivation of the electron, the gene, and the computer chip.

The effect of these outer influences is noticeable. Our children are prematurely hardened; wizened but not wise. Within those precocious children, however, the unfolding of human soul forces proceeds sequentially, and although the children may be growing up faster, hurried by premature fears and expectations, the essential fifth grader is still a fifth grader, poised on the brink of impending adolescence. He may express himself less agreeably than his counterpart of thirty years ago, but if the Waldorf teacher addresses the part of the child which it has always been the Waldorf teacher's privilege to address, namely the individuality of the child, then today's child will listen just as avidly to tales of wily Zeus, as the teacher himself might have done a generation ago.

Fifth graders are about eleven years old and have been since the inception of the first Waldorf school in 1921. Although children do start school at ever younger ages, the Waldorf schools have managed to preserve the child as a kindergartner until s/he is approaching age seven. Thus, Waldorf children predictably reach the moment of inner development when the beginning of the science curriculum and the replacement of myth and legend with the history of men on earth is appropriate, in fifth grade. Now they listen in fascination to the story of Prometheus, learn about fungi, ferns and cotyledons, and map the differing terrains of their homeland. The fifth grade curriculum still meets the fifth graders with substance appropriate to their evolution through the grades. Whether born in 1981 or in 1951, they are born into the challenge of the consciousness soul in the twentieth century; twentieth century children born in the atomic age. Their evolution still follows a discernible pattern. But because the children are prone to our century's hardening influences — over–stimulation, premature intellectualization — the pattern may be less easily discernible. It is up to the teacher to find it. For beneath the hardening armour of sophistication, the embryo ego is already active. And now more than ever, the Waldorf teacher's task is to provide that individuality with a scaffold that properly supports its incarnation. That, after all, is the task of the Waldorf teacher, whether in kindergarten, the grades or high school: to support and strengthen through proper exercise the physical, etheric and astral bodies, so that when the ego does at last emerge at about twenty–one, it can meet the hardening world without having to resort to hardness itself as an impenetrable, self–defensive, self–imprisoning barricade.

That emerging ego, emerging ever so tenderly in even the youngest child, and still relatively primitive in the brash adolescent, and sometimes not quite hatched even in the full–fledged adult, is the infant member of humanity's evolution, as well as the infant waiting to be born only after the child leaves school. This inner kernel of the child, this as–yet–unexpressed (or mis–expressed) core of individuality in the child, is what the Waldorf teacher must constantly address. In the kindergarten, this mysteriously eternal maturing aspect of the developing child is best met through the teacher's gestures and movements, i.e. by appealing primarily to the child's physical body; in grade school, through story–picture, form, rhythm, i.e. primarily through the etheric body; in the high school, the approach must be through the students' consciousness, that is, through the astral body. That is what the Waldorf teacher can learn to do. He can learn to approach the child appropriately. To do so, the teacher's every sense must be keenly honed to grasp both the expected development and the unexpected individuality being born.

The teacher can prepare himself to recognize the expected changes. He can study Rudolf Steiner's lectures on child development so that he can learn to recognize the awesome evolution, so dynamic yet so subtle, undergone by every child. He can immerse himself in the curriculum and learn to draw upon his own creative capacities as he strives to develop the latent imaginative, inspirative and intuitive forces by means of which he may bring that curriculum to life. But what does the teacher learn to recognize the individuality embedded in the growing child? And how can the teacher anticipate the world matrix within which the child born today will stand as a fifth grader eleven years from now?

Seniors graduating from high school this year were born about 1974. That was the year that Nixon resigned, Patty Hearst was abducted and Solzhenitsyn was exiled. Children born this year will enter first grade about 1999, they will be fifth graders in 2003 and will leave school around the year 2010. Would we have anticipated, when the current crop of graduates was born in 1974, that the year of their school–leaving, 1992, would look the way it does? Can we look ahead for the graduating class of 2010 with any reasonable prophecies? For what kind of a world are we preparing our children?

How can we prepare them? How can we prepare ourselves to guide them? Can we prepare ourselves for the world they are facing?

Before attempting answers to these daunting questions, let us consider again the realms of change challenging the teacher: the child is changing, the teacher is changing, the world is changing. The child and the teacher are changing in more or less discernible seven year cycles. The world is changing in ways which indicate a direction, if not a pattern: technology is on the rise and in its wake the value of the human being is diminished.

The child is not the only one getting swept into this cold gust. The teacher, too, is vulnerable. And it is the teacher, also, who, faced with a hardening world, finds himself growing crusty, unable to refurbish the forces of dedication he needs to carry on with his task, embattled as he is.

In the United States, lack of enrolment is a critical problem for many schools. An even greater problem is the shortage of Waldorf teachers — Waldorf teachers, not merely teachers who've been through a two year training, or are looking to establish a school for their own children, or who have been kindled by the short flame of momentary and sentimental idealism.

Waldorf children on the other hand, abound. All children are potentially Waldorf children. With some, though, the ones who seem to have had serious pre-earthy intentions of finding their Waldorf school, one senses that in the school they have found their true home. These are the children who, whether they enter the Waldorf school at seven or seventeen, know they have found their home. Their parents know it, and so do their teachers. Such children have perhaps been spared a premature awakening; or perhaps there are other circumstances that have allowed them to grow up naturally so that they are neither hardened nor sophisticated. If they enter the school in a later grade, they may appreciate their new school just because it is so different from what they have known. These are the people whose school years as Waldorf children may enable them to preserve their souls in spite of the influences from without. The world, however, cannot be kept at bay, and a lovely eleven year old — pliable, artistic, enthusiastic — may, in later adolescence, face the gravest dangers. Then the child's most important teacher will be his own higher self, the self which the class teacher activated.

Whereas the teacher's greatest ally is the curriculum, the child's protector and preserver in his love for his teacher. Children want to love their teachers. It is not by chance that the one question Rudolf Steiner was sure to ask the children whenever he visited the Waldorf School was, "Do you love your teachers?" And the children always responded with a resounding, "Yes!" Today, too, although there is no one with sufficient transcendence to ask the question, the inner stance of the children must be the same. This love of the child for his teacher, which is the foundation for all Waldorf teaching, rests upon the teacher's inner life.

If the teacher is inwardly centred, if though spiritual activity he strives to find balance in his soul, he will merit the children's love, he will experience that love as a strength, and further, he will cultivate the capacities to meet the mad pace of world events.

But this spiritual activity, this balance in the soul, these are no easy matter. There is no prescription, and every student of anthroposophy knows the enormity of the struggle for inner harmony and consequent inner activity. What distinguishes the particular challenge confronting the teacher is, of course, the presence of the children. And would they be children if theirs were always a comforting, harmonizing presence? Yet that is just the part of them that we must have steadily in view if we are to meet the demands of the fast approaching end of this century. It is the part of them that cannot always be seen with the outer eye, but it can be seen with the inner eye. We can begin to notice, to see, to hear what is latent in the children if at the same time we can tend what is latent in ourselves: our full humanity.

Already present in the children is the future they incarnated into. It is up to us to strengthen what they have brought along, to give it a chance to grow, to nurture it. And what is it? It is their I. That I is ready for the future. It has been prepared for the future. It can teach us about the future if we meet it with our own striving ego. The interplay between child and teacher is powerfully delicate. An astonishing sensitivity resonates between them. But the teacher is grown-up. The initiative for setting standards must come from him. If he can harness his inner life, then the child can show him the way. It will be up to the teacher to replenish his own connection to his inner life again and again, on a daily, even hourly, basis. Whether he attempts this on the basis of cultivation of the meditative life, cultivation of the arts, cultivation of a rhythmical life, or on the basis of any of the particular studies and exercises Rudolf Steiner left as legacy, the teacher's on-going striving to revitalize that connection will address the children more directly than anything else. The child's inner life is immediately addressed by the teacher's inner life. The teacher, having once discerned the child's inner response, usually ever so much subtler than the outer behaviour, will find himself encouraged and enthused and able to penetrate the future because he is able to stand fully in the child's presence.

Mystery Play is Now

In an interview with Andrew Wolpert, Christopher Marcus describes some of the challenges he has faced directing Rudolf Steiner's Mystery Dramas in English. His production of The Guardian of the Threshold *is currently on tour.*

AW: How does working with the Mystery Dramas relate to the theme of coping with the accelerated pace of change?

CM: First of all I think that is a very dangerous question. If an anthroposophist has to ask himself. "How do I cope with the speed of change?" that is quite tragic, in so far as anthroposophy is living in the Being of change. That means living in the revelation of Michael, living now, working towards the consequences of his deeds which he does now, and he should not have to consider change — change should be inherent in his Being, everyday. It is something we have to deal with everyday, again and again and again. How can I be in my own being an anarchist? How can I overcome my own tendency of wanting to have the answers? Saying, "Oh, it's like this. Oh, it's like that. I've got the answer to this. I've got the answer to that." Whereas in fact I am continually, from out of anthroposophy, struggling to ask questions and not find the answers. The question is, "How can I do a deed in the power of Michael?" Michael being the Spirit of the Time. How can I not be frightened that the people living in the past, who conserve the forms, will judge what I do? To do what I think is right in this moment. How can I do a deed and not be frightened that the consequences of my deed will be wrong?

These are two ideas which create fear. One is that what I do is going to be wrong — I'm going to bang my head against a wall, I'm going to make a mistake, so I won't do it. The other is that I won't do it because I'm frightened that people who conserve the forms of how–things–should–be will judge it as being wrong. And these are two fears which for an artist are absolutely deadly. Because it means that I can't listen to the moment. I can't listen to the truth of the meeting. I can't listen to the truth of the questions arising every second of the day.

I think that, if one talks in anthroposophical terminology, we have great problems in England where we can say that the powers of Gabriel are still very strong — the communal understanding, the social aspect (we do things together) — high wonderful qualities, but it's still very strongly out of the Gabriel forces. Being kind to each other. Being social. Don't hurt the other too much. Be diplomatic.

In Holland, where I work, we have got Raphael. Raphael is the Spirit of healing. There the tendency is to think that we are all sick. We are all ill. We have got to heal each other. You've got the therapies, and all of that sort of thing. But the Time Spirit of now, we know, is Michael, and Gabriel and Raphael have to serve Michael, and I very often have the feeling that it's as if these two mighty Beings have not given up their power. So the tendency is that we start using anthroposophy, note the word using anthroposophy, in order to heal, in order to create certain social forms. And of course that is totally legitimate. But the fact is that anthroposophy is no set of codes, is not a set of norms. Anthroposophy is living in the moment, is something you could say is intensely artistic.

One of the aspects of art, one of the main driving forces of art is "How can I be true to my inner impulses as I experience them this moment now?" As I said in the beginning, not as I feel I ought to do it, not because of what is expected of me, but as the spiritual entity of the play reveals it to me in relationship to the actors, in relationship to the person who makes the scenery, in relationship with the light. In the interaction of these artists together you have an intuition, at that moment. And that intuition you put on the stage.

AW: That shows the need to be aware of the stream of constantly changing phenomena. I wonder, are there examples, specifically from your work with the Mystery Play, where you experienced that pull of old form in one direction and fear of people's expectations in another, and yet perceived a true archetype that can live out of the past and into the future taking appropriate new forms?

CM: That is very well formulated. I don't know if I can answer it so easily.

AW: We don't necessarily have to get into criticisms of your production but never the less, there must be areas where you feel, "I've got to do it this way because although there are accepted ways of doing it, the real demands of this situation are different. And yet there is a true archetype that I have not lost sight of." Is that polarity something you can give examples of or speak generally about?

CM: I'll try to describe two things. One is that, as a director, I am continually trying to experience the archetype. The archetype of the Mystery Play is not something that in the first place I can see as a mental image. An imagination is something that you experience with your inner eye, you hear it if it goes more towards the intuitional side of things, you experience it as a dynamic, and I certainly would not claim to be able to perceive in the sense of *Knowledge of the Higher Worlds*, the imagination of let's say, *The Challenge of the Soul (The Soul's Probation)*. But what I could say is that if I close my eyes I am capable of seeing the play as a whole. By moving towards understanding the play as a whole, and at the moment when I experience something in relationship to the actors and the scenery, there are a large number of different

ways in which a scene could reveal itself. In relationship to
that, for example, I don't think that the spiritual world has to
necessarily reveal itself behind a scrim, a gauze. I think it is
possible to allow the actors' space to be used in such a way as,
for example, when the spirit of Benedictus appears in the
Middle Ages. As a spirit, he usually speaks from behind the
scrim, and a monk in the castle hears that, and he is frightened. So we have the spiritual world behind a sort of gauze,
and the physical world in front. I think that that is a limited
way of dealing with the spiritual world. I think that if one has
an imagination, a vision or a dream — dreams are so incred-
ibly strong, so overpowering that it is around you, it is in you,
you are part of it. And that's why I chose that Benedictus steps
out of the back space and walks around. The monk is lying on
the floor moving in certain geometrical forms, a certain pattern
so that a ritualistic aspects comes into it.

That's one aspect. Another example is dealing with Lucifer
and Ahriman or Astrid, Philia and Luna. I don't think it is
necessarily correct to have the speakers off stage and only the
eurythmy on stage. I think the speakers being on stage create
a space, create a character which could be the mental image
of the person who is having the imagination, who is having
the spiritual experience. The eurythmy depicts forces that
stream out into the cosmos. There are things that in normal
dealings with the Mystery Plays aren't done.

AW: When you say "normal" you mean hitherto conventional?

CM: Yes, that's right. And I feel that the production that I
have done is unbelievably conventional.

AW: The two instances that you have given now of having
the speakers and the eurythmy together and getting away
from the scrim seemed to me, if I have understood you
rightly, examples of how, from a spiritually scientific point

of view you have overcome a kind of dualism. Are there other examples where you know that an audience's expectation today when they come to the theatre, even to see a Mystery Play by Rudolf Steiner, places you under a certain urgency — inclines you to make other changes?

CM: Yes, very much so. I think that one of the main things, the greatest battle, is the actual acting. Acting out of what certain characters feel. I think that that is almost one of the most important things. Johannes Thomasius, Strader or Cap-esius, or Maria for that matter, go through absolutely awful crises, incredible crises. They have breakdowns. And I feel that reciting the breakdown, and sticking to a certain form, in no way depicts the degree of crisis the character is going through. And I think the actors must be able to scream and wail or yell their problem, in the most exoteric way that you can imagine. You can't get that bad enough, you can't be dramatic enough. There has been a fear of showing the subjective nature on stage until now, because a Mystery Play mustn't be subjective. I feel that that is a big mistake, because it is a drama. It is a Mystery Drama, by all means, but it is a drama which means that the most intimate passions, hates and loves of a certain character who has gone through tremendous crises, have to be enacted in a way that the audience are, as much as possible, really gripped. And that's also an example of where we are only just scratching the surface. And finding actors, or enabling actors to play these emotions without becoming common or garden screaming and yelling, because you have to find a style in which it can reveal itself. I think the Mystery Plays are very, very shocking, and they are not nice and veiled, as it were, clichéd homely dramas. They are very, very shocking, earth shattering dramas and I think they should be dealt with as such.

AW: Is this development that you're describing now a con-cession to the sensationalism of modern life, or is it to achieve greater integrity in the approach to the drama itself anyway?

CM: You can't possibly come into the essence of the drama if you don't realize the human element that is inherent in these plays. It is very, very, very human. With all the most awful things that can happen to us — they are all in the dramas. And I think a modern audience has to be able to relate to that. No normal film or modern drama, where emotions are shown, however well they are done, can be compared to the sort of crisis that a character comes into if they are going through a spiritual crisis, and you get that on the stage.

AW: What can you say in connection with the language? Were there struggles doing it in English, with a particular translation? Is the English language aspect of the work something that you can throw light on?

CM: I would almost go so far as to say, and it is very naughty to say this, that I think the Mystery Plays are better in English than in German.

AW: I think anthroposophy is sometimes better in English than in German.

CM: Ha, ha, ha. Well, I wouldn't go so far as to say that, but I certainly would as far as the arts are concerned. You see Steiner had to come to certain formulations of truth, of exactness in order to be able to unite thoughts that he experienced with the German word. And we, as English people translating it, have to deal much more with the fluidity of what is around the word — the emotions, the sub-text, so that we have more words to express the same thought, which means that it is much, much more dramatic. It gives the actor then a possibility because the actor takes part in the act of translating the text, and because the actor is not the translator, the actor is the person who for months on end has been living into the character, his character. Being English, will help him find the right ways to express the thoughts that he can have by thinking the text, which is Steiner's text. So there is a closer interaction between the artist with an English folksoul and the writer who has a German folksoul, so it becomes much more organic and whole. And for me, as a director, then there are more possibilities staging something in English than the German director would have.

You see a modern German production must adhere faithfully to the original text, of course. However, a translation allows us to get away from the inevitably dated idiom of Steiner's German, so that the language is not a barrier. A German director is not free to "remove" the obstacle of "old-fashioned" language. We want the timeless content to speak to people today in the best contemporary idiom.

AW: Are you saying that in English today one can achieve something that is closer artistically to Steiner's intention than the German can make possibly?

CM: I think that that is a very dangerous statement. I wouldn't dare to say that, but what I would dare to say is, that in Germany you've got the upholding of a tradition of how it has to be staged, what Marie Steiner did based on what Rudolf Steiner had said. That means that if anyone directs the play in the Goetheanum, for example, they do it out of that fundamental memory of what Rudolf or Marie Steiner did. This is the crux of the matter. However right and however good it may be, it is always an attempt to do a very good copy of what was done there. And as an artist I can not copy. So in the sense that Rudolf Steiner is trying to create a new art, which is creating out of the moment in relationship to his being then, living in the Time Spirit of 1992. How does that Time Spirit deal with the spiritual content of the Mystery Plays now? Not having the ballast of having to do it as it was done. I would dare to say "yes" to your question. Through doing the English now, we have the possibility of coming to a more creative revelation of the Mystery Plays than they have in Germany. Do you follow?

AW: I do, and I am delighted to hear it. Is that because the act of translating requires such a degree of conscious responsibility that if one were doing it in French, Italian or any other language, that would also be true, or is it because, as you suggested earlier, there are things about the English language that particularly favour that development? Is it the getting away from German only, or is it also the getting into English?

CM: I think the getting away from the German is fundamental. I think that is number one. The other factor is that the English has got this extraordinary consciousness–soul which reveals itself in its dramatic heritage. And the English language is particularly internationally seen as being the language for drama. It has got to do with holding back, not saying how things are. That's where drama is. Drama exists in the tension between truth and lies. Reality and irreality, illusion. This is related to the English folksoul — the looking at things, the onlooker; and because the English folk, as people, have this inherent acting ability which all nations recognize. The English actor is just an actor. You have got brilliant actors in Germany and Holland etc. but there is something that the English actor has which the other people haven't. It has to do with the English folksoul.

I would very much like to direct the four Mystery Plays as a block and take them to New Zealand, South Africa, America, Australia, and I think that anthroposophy via the Mystery Plays, via the English language, not French, German, Dutch but particularly through the English language, has the ability to reach an absolutely starving, English–speaking audience.

AW: Although you've made these remarks now particularly in connection with drama, my heart is warmed by what you say because I have a strong sense that actually what you've said is true of anthroposophical endeavours beyond drama. And it's not just to get away from the German, it is also because it is possible to do things in the English language that actually complete what was started in German. Much of the burden we feel by the German way of doing things in the English anthroposophical world is not just difficult for us, but I sense also that it is actually very retarding for Germany and for German anthroposophists. If we can wean ourselves off that dependence, then also German anthroposophy will be liberated to go on to its next stage.

CM: I think that is very wise. Yes, I would agree with that, although I would add that I think that fundamentally we are in a situation where I don't think it's about copying Germany, it has not been about copying Germany for quite some time.

The difficulty lies in England, for example, in overcoming the phlegmatic nature. If you have got an idea, do it! Put it into practice! There is this pragmatic nature that we have here which is, "Well, I don't know, maybe we will, or maybe we should ..." And we sit down and talk about it and nothing happens. You could say it is a lack of confidence, a real lack of confidence in the English folk soul and what it can do. So if we don't give into the water that always goes back into the ocean, but goes forward through the intellectual capacity of the English folk soul, through the English language, through its exactness, through its gentleness, through its subtlety, through its musicality, through its dramatic qualities, then it should be able to achieve for Spiritual Science what the German language can't achieve because it is isolated, especially because of the tragedy of European history since Steiner's time.

Those who are born into the English language should love that which German brought forth, the tremendous consciousness and tremendous spirituality — the development of the I.

That is not happening enough. And also we are conservative in our nature, and we are not listening enough to our indignation as to what tradition is. That indignation that we have is actually something which is right. "Now we're going to go on and we're going to do it. Who's going to do it?" Not who's going to talk about it — who is going to do it? And I feel that is something that the English really should strongly develop because they have tremendous powers of adaptation. There is no country like England that is good at adaptation, understanding other people, adapting and going forwards. And our tendency now is to shelter, we want to protect ourselves, shield ourselves from the world, and that is tragic. I think that is tragic.

AW: In what sense do the metamorphosed Mystery Dramas, metamorphosed through all the processes that you have described, really have something to say first of all to anthroposophists today who may well already be familiar with the content, but also to newcomers to anthroposophy?

CM: For anthroposophists I think the Mystery Plays fundamentally are a lesson in coming to terms with that karmic stream they belong to, and overcoming the differences in opinion as to how something should be done. Through seeing the karmic heritage that they have, through so working together at anthroposophy, working together out of the Sun Mysteries they unite the different karmic streams. All to often in anthroposophical movements the initiative can't move forward because within the initiative you have got two polarized points of view, or two polarized karmic streams, and they are so busy trying to understand each other, not understanding each other, that the initiative as a will impulse can't move forward. I think the Mystery Play is fundamentally a lesson in understanding karma. Community karma, group karma, family karma, individual karma, what are we on earth for at all? That is one thing.

For people who are not familiar with anthroposophy I think it is mapping out, bringing words, formulating, bringing in picture form the unconscious questions that are asked through being confronted with spiritual experiences, either consciously or unconsciously. Spiritual experiences in the sense of crossing the threshold, through crises, through nervous breakdowns, through not understanding life situations that they are dealing with. Dreams, drugs, religion, science, spiritual things as it were smashed through the layers of wakeful consciousness and create doubt in one's being. The Mystery Plays are able to map out the path that one can take and give new perspectives in life.

AW: But is that particularly so today? Has the need for that in the last seventy year become greater? Has the scope for that, through drama, become greater?

CM: Look at the amount of films that there are about reincarnation and karma. It is quite extraordinary, but they don't often answer questions. They give a distorted view of what this occult truth is, more now than ever. Reincarnation and karma are spoken about everywhere — it is a normal phenomenon. It is becoming so normal that it is becoming cliché, and I think the Mystery Play, as a cultural factor, should be entertained in such a way that it is normal, it is part of our heritage.

Mystery Play is now. Mystery Play is not 1913. Mystery Play is an absolute necessity. It is what we are all about. I feel very strongly that we are open to that now — everyone is asking a question, and it is our fault, it is our problem. "How can we bring that into society in a way that is normal and not a sect, not a hidden thing for initiates only, that belong to a certain society?" It belongs to mankind, and that is our task.

Regenerative Grammar

Andrew Wolpert

The degenerative forces in language threaten to change us. The mindless slavery to pre-cast thought forms in stock phrases, the ascendancy of the lowest linguistic common denominator, careless and inexact use of language, and obfuscating style are all ever more evident. Yet they also increasingly provoke intelligently reasoned and widely supported protests, and it is heartening that these instances of "fallen" language do not go unchallenged. The purpose of this article, however, is to identify a resurrection process in our use of language that is not a symptomatic reaction, but that develops out of our inborn devotion to the sovereignty of meaning.

This fundamental commitment to significance is by its very nature not a static condition, but a process that we can most directly observe in our use of language. Here we can distinguish a series of six separate stages, each of which contributes an essential element. At the first level we find words, written or spoken, that make up the sense-perceptible dimension of language, where the Logos finally materializes into an optical or acoustic stimulus. If we trace this process of incarnation back, we next come to the second level where we recognize that these verbal components are governed by a structure of grammar that consists of categories (such as verbs, nouns, and so on) and laws by which they can be brought into relation with each other. Thirdly we come to the level where we discern the forces of change that affect the grammatical structures and the words themselves. In English these changes are most evident in the process of grammatical simplification and enrichment of vocabulary. These two tendencies have combined to provide a language which has lost most of the richness of the inflected form of verbs and nouns, and certain other structural subtleties, but which, on the other hand, places an immense wealth of words at the disposal of the speaker.

The fourth level has to do with our personal predilection for using certain words or phrases, our largely unconscious expression of our personality in the way we speak or write. The fifth stage is where we are conscious of the will to express and of the intention to communicate. This has to do with our grasp of something meaningful which is therefore worth articulating, either to ourselves in language–based thinking, or to others in thinking–based language. This "something meaningful" apprehended at the fifth stage derives from the sixth level that is the realm of the Logos.

These stages have very different qualities. The Logos is universal, in contrast to the very individual ego experience of the desire to communicate. That which characterizes our personal language predilections is the possibility of becoming conscious of these initially rather unconscious effects of our soul life. The forces of change attest to that which is living as the organic life–forces. In contrast to this, but not in contradiction, we can observe how the structure of grammar displays many symptoms of dying. The defiance of the grammatical conventions by the cultures of Black English, modern poetry, American rap, and English street idiom, and the tacit acceptance of the unconsciously unconventional grammar of other ethnic forms of English all point to this dying process. The shifts that are taking place within certain grammatical concepts are less easily noticed, and it is also more difficult to say whether they are further evidence of this disintegration or whether they arise out of the organic forces of living change. The words at the last level, the audible or visible crystallizations of the Logos are in themselves dead. Often beautiful as a crystal is, often evocative of the magnificent life that gave rise to them, and often precious in their service to a living meaning, they are, nevertheless, lifeless.

The Logos	(the universal)
The Will to Communicate	(the individual)
Personal Language Predilections	(the becoming conscious)
Forces of Change in Language	(the living)
Grammar	(the dying)
Words	(the dead)

If this were the whole story it would be destined for an un-happy ending. If the expression of the Logos were inevitably bound to a dying language, then the degenerative forces described in the first paragraph would easily prevail over the way language changes, over our personal modes of expression, and even over our will to say anything. While it is true that language has a particular role to play in our thinking process, and that words in a certain way contribute to the shaping of our concepts, a moment's honest reflection on our own cognitive process can leave us in no doubt that our words do not determine our thinking. If thinking is the ego activity in which an individual is conscious, free, and responsible, then it is a process that depends on language even though it may have emancipated itself from words.

Nevertheless, it is salutary to be aware of how words can appear to imprison one's thinking. An inappropriately restricted concept attached to a word can prevent a necessary connection from being made in one's cognitive process. If, for example, one thinks that the word "science" refers to a field, and furthermore by convention to the field of nature accessible only to our five senses, then it is impossible to understand that anthroposophy can legitimately be thought of as spiritual science. Clearly, however, it is not the word "science" that is blocking a connection, it is not even the "wrong" concept that is restricting the thinking. It is actually the unwillingness to let go of or broaden the inadequate concept. In order for that reluctance to melt away, one has to have the experience of science being a method of inquiry rather than a field of inquiry. This necessary experience can either come directly in the effort to make sense of an event, or indirectly through another person's explanation based on an agreed shared initial concept. In either case the solution to the difficulty apparently caused by the words, in fact lies in the realm of the ego activity as it individualizes what it grasps from the universal Logos. Though the particular Logos substance that is being won in this individualizing process may as yet have no corresponding signifier at the level of words, the process by which it is recognized and incarnated into old words redefined, or newly coined ones, is itself entirely language dependent.

It is in this thinking–language structuring of the ego, in this individualized Logos activity, that our devotion to meaning is enshrined. The intention to communicate what arises here is impelled by the love of the truth. This initiates a process that we can consciously carry through our predilections, through the forces that change language, into the disintegrating structure of grammar, and even down into the lifeless words. This process can be described more fully at each of the four stages.

The possibility of becoming aware of how our language predilections influence our idiom means that instead of merely allowing the way we speak to express something of our personality, we can more consciously use language that serves what we want to say. Such a transformation goes together with bringing order into one's soul life. The already prevalent distaste for clichés and meaningless "user–friendly" euphemisms shows how very awake we are at this level. The predilections of our unconscious emotional, social, political, or commercialized patterns of behaviour are often dishonest. The statement "Thank you for travelling with us" is usually made on the dubious advice of a public relations expert, by an employee who feels not the least bit of gratitude, to a passen-ger who may have had no choice in selecting the airline or railway company, and who in any case is not fooled by the words. The linguistic means of expressing gratitude are eroded by this abuse. It may be a good thing that it takes some courage to say "I love you," but the reason for that is in no small measure the fear that the accumulation of over-use and misuse will threaten credibility. "This car park is temporarily full." Of course those cars are not going to remain there for ever, and the valuable adverb "temporarily" is used to function in a devalued way as an unnecessary and insincere apology for a condition that is in any case devoid of blame.

Certainly grammatical structures and words have long been used for expressing nuances and attitudes beyond their surface function. The whole rich culture of irony and the English institution of the understatement depend on such creative and imaginative use of language. It is the unconscious or indolent behaviour in this area that is so offensive, and the increasing opprobrium it causes, shows how far we have already come in our awareness of the value of saying what we mean. It is this fidelity to the Logos that has the power to change our bad habits.

When we observe how the spiritual, cultural, historical, and social forces of change have shaped our language, we can recognize how a "simplified" grammar and an enriched vocabulary are precisely the conditions that challenge the ego to express itself both efficiently and beautifully. (For a fuller discussion of this point see "Are We Detached?" *The Golden Blade,* 1992). In this context we must consider the creative genius of modern American English. We are familiar with the horrors of Disneyspeak, and with ludicrous forms such as "zero–water–retention–capability" to describe a bucket that leaks. On the other hand, what is less often noticed is that particularly spoken American usage has an urgent pulse of immediacy and freshness that is vital and sometimes volatile, and that serves communication both honestly and aesthetically. The expression "to ride the road" can be a rather wordily explained as driving round a curve with the minimum steering that visibility and the presence of other traffic allow. The odious and often absurd politicking behind the phenomenon of Politically Correct speech, and the coercive and even aggressive evangelism it inspires, should not blind us to the significance of such consciously channelled forces of change in the service of meaning. Conscientious attention to our integrity in this area is a sure means of cultivating the faculties of discernment and healthy discrimination needed to harness the forces of change in the service of the Logos.

It is the same reverence for what we really want to say that must stand behind our efforts to combat sloppy or "ungrammatical" usage. Teaching children correct grammar will not of itself improve their command of the language. Grammar is an expression of the Logos. The need for clear and efficient grammatical forms will be unavoidable when clear thinking, that is also an expression of the Logos, demands commensurately clear means of expression. The quality of what wants to be expressed will determine the mode of expression. Here one can truly speak of grammar regeneration out of devotion to the source of grammar: the reverence for meaning that lives in the Logos. At this level we are not interested in vain attempts to rescue the distinction between "who" and "whom," and we recognize that putting a preposition at the end of a sentence is not something to worry about. The spiritual regeneration of grammar consists of living consciously in the meaning of the structures we use. Language teachers and translators are immediately aware of this, but the reverence for the word that every meditant, parent, and simply conscious language user develops, leads to this awakening to the Logos in the structure of language. The dying grammar is reconstituted in the consciousness of the language user. This is regenerative grammar.

But there is a final stage. The renewing process described above can be known to us only because we incarnate it into words. The dead words serve as the mirror that reflects this living reality back to our consciousness. It is perhaps not so easy to distinguish the grammar from the words because it is the configuration of the latter that makes the former visible. However, the grammar exists as an expression of the Logos independently of the words that then manifest and material-ize it. In Chapter 9 of *The Philosophy Of Freedom* Rudolf Steiner describes the bodily constitution as giving us our ego consciousness, but not, of course, as bearing the ego. In addition, the ego consciousness can emancipate itself from the bodily constitution once the ego consciousness has been taken up by the ego. Herein lies the key to the paradox of what is wordless, but not language–free, thinking. Words give us the awareness of the grammar they reflect. That grammar is the structuring activity of the Logos which manifests in thinking. Thinking can free itself from the words, but as an ego activity that is dedicated to meaning, it lives in the Logos structuring of language, even though it may cease to need words.

This reference to the bodily constitution is not made because it is a helpful, analogous comparison, but because of its exact congruity. The redemption of humanity depends on the Logos having incarnated right into the bodily constitution of a human being. It would not have been sufficient for Christ to unite himself with the spiritual part of fallen humanity. The spiritual resurrection depended on the Logos becoming flesh. What Rudolf Steiner describes in this connection in the lecture cycle given in Karlsruhe in 1911, *From Jesus To Christ*, depends on the essential distinction between the physical body laid down in Old Saturn, and the material flesh connected with the fall in Lemuria. In the regeneration of grammar we are no more concerned to save words than Christ was the save the flesh of Jesus. Like the flesh, words can fall away when they have served their reflecting purpose. It was the spiritual form and the formative spirit of the physical body that rose renewed on Easter Sunday, and it is the formative structuring faculty in the thinking that is resurrected by regenerative grammar. This affirms our human inseparability from meaning. This is a cognitive confirmation of our spiritual origin and destiny.

Losing Ground

Ria Freiermuth

Educated in Germany and South Africa, Ria Freiermuth built up and ran a successful business in South Africa for some years. Last year she felt the time had come for a change, though quite what this might be was not clear. She sold the business and came to England where she attended courses at the Centre for Social Development. Though much has been experienced inwardly, the next step is not yet apparent. Currently in her mid–thirties, she describes below the testing moments one can experience in the process of thorough reappraisal, leading possibly to radical changes in one's working life.

"Yes, I know what you are saying to me; but, I have really nothing to say — nothing; I feel so utterly empty." ... "Alright, I shall try again over the weekend." —

And ...

Again emptiness.

I remember the old vedantic (Indian) lines,

"It was not then non–being but not being ..."

A contradiction for the modern reasoning mind. Yet, this is how I experience my being at this present stage in my life. Suddenly, time has stopped within me.

A complete standstill.

Nothing is moving if I do not move it.

I am free — boundlessly free:

No home, no country, no work, no dependants — no call — no direction.

Complete openness, vastness, stillness.
And yet, decisions have to be made. Where do I go next?
I tried some avenues but the echo is slow, undefined.
One promising Yes turned into a sudden NO.
Disappointment — despair.
There is no ground under my feet any more.
I keep going, resisting the laming force trying to paralyse me.
I am frightfully free — yet, bound.

What happened outwardly up to now was just a reflection of an inner process. I had turned away from a thriving business, had had to overcome many obstacles in order to leave on a sabbatical from a so-called "third-world" country which I loved dearly. I was motivated by a deep inner longing for the Nordic light and culture, by the will to find people who carry similar social impulses.

At first, Europe was a culture shock to me after having been away for so many years. I travelled around trying to make contacts. I joined courses to deepen and school my understanding of the human being and of myself. At the same time, allowing myself to get in touch again with the European mind, and to meet people from all over the world.

However, my inner loneliness grew, feeling a stranger without country, without home, without job; Who was I?

Human relationships brought disappointments and need to be worked through. It seems easy to walk away, but friendship and love need to be practised.

Consciously I had given up all earthly belongings, status, financial security; I had left my familiar surroundings, my acquaintances, my friends. I myself created the situation I find myself in. The question of truth and faithfulness is becoming more pertinent than ever before.

I remember the words of Dr Mees at a workshop in Driebergen, Holland, many years ago. He had asked the question, "Who am I?" "Well," he said, "I am DOCTOR MEES. I have a certain social status and thus, enjoy prestige. I have a house, a wife, children, a car, a bank account, and the Bank Manager knows me, DOCTOR MEES, well. I am a Dutchman, and ..., and ... I am 'sooo' big" (he drew with his arms a wide circular line around him).

"And you, Mrs X," he continued, "you are the wife of Mr X, you are this and that, and you, too, are 'sooo' big. Yes, we are both 'sooo' big that we can't reach each other! But let's say we cut off all these layers of our personality; what will remain? — The Little Prince that lives in all of us."

The Little Prince lives in all of us, wanting to shine forth. I know this. And in the dreadful moments of utter darkness, loneliness, and powerlessness I remember the Little Prince in me, in others.

He is waiting to shine through me, to find his brothers in the encounters with the others. He is waiting for me to release him.

How could I want to release him without the experience that he is there? How could I want to set him free without understanding what it means to be trapped, isolated, powerless, yet, full of strength and free; ignorant, yet, full of knowledge and wisdom? And I recognize that the Little Prince is waiting and longing to be revealed; that I need patience and persistence, inner activity and the continuous awareness that the Little Prince can stand on his own ground. To be a "no–body" in the world of "bodies," stirs the wish to become "some-body." In finding the Little Prince you lose "every body."

To acknowledge and be the Little Prince inspires the striving to penetrate darkness on the way towards becoming a true human being. This is giving you the substance for the building of the new ground to stand and walk on. The path is paved by pearls of tears of powerlessness, disillusionment, disappointment, vulnerability. The light on this path is created by the power of truth and inner faithfulness to the guidance of the spiritual beings, to MICHAEL, to CHRIST in Man. And I keep going on ...

Finding One's Place — the transformation of employment

Stephen Briault

A colleague once told me about the phase of his life after leaving Emerson College in the early seventies.

"It took us a while to find our place," he said. "Actually, my wife didn't even know there was such a thing as finding your place. She thought people just had jobs ..."

Many of us, now in the lunchtime or early afternoon of our lives, have been looking for our place — our work and its context — ever since that period. Sometimes we seem to find it — for a time. Then doubts or difficulties occur; we feel restless; often we move on, seeking perhaps more congenial colleagues, more autonomy, more creative tasks, a situation which allows us to pursue what we see as our individual purpose or destiny.

The world of work is undergoing considerable turmoil today, and this seems likely to continue or intensify over the coming decades. The turmoil is not only to do with unemployment, but also over-employment, stress, motivation and values. It manifests in individuals and also societal trends. This article attempts to sketch some of the phenomena relating to this changing area of our lives, and to suggest some orientation points which may be helpful.

* * *

Over seven or eight years of running "Questions in Mid-career" seminars, and counselling individual clients from a wide range of backgrounds, I have observed two main patterns in people struggling with career issues, which I believe relate to the polarity of thought and will.

Feeling stuck

Firstly, there are those who feel "stuck." Often these people have been initially quite successful in their profession and achieved much in their twenties and thirties. Many things are often taken for granted during this period. Work-values are not radically questioned. The conventional career path is assumed to be appropriate. The demands of job, family, mortgage suppress any underlying doubts. This pattern is also observable, incidentally, for people in "idealistic" professions such as therapeutic or educational work: the goals are somewhat different, but the phenomena of over-dedication to assumed values can be very similar.

The "stuck" feelings arise from a growing, eventually unavoidable perception that something is missing, and/or that one's own development is no longer being supported and stimulated by the demands of the work. "I'm starting to repeat myself," people in this situation say, "I need to move on — but I don't know how or where. This kind of work is all I know, all I'm good at ..." Such individuals usually understand their own situation quite well. They know *why* they feel stuck — but they also have a collection of very good reasons why they cannot do much about it. Both their outer circumstances and their established habits produce an inertia which takes tremendous effort to overcome.

People in this state may fantasize for years about making a radical change in their working lives; often it takes a strong "external" factor — usually redundancy, or perhaps an intense conflict with colleagues — to provoke an actual change. When this occurs, identity-threatening anxieties may be provoked.

The person will need to draw on all their inner resources of courage, self-esteem and imagination in order to face this sudden challenge creatively, and not resort to panic measures in an attempt to re-establish the former status quo. They will also need social and personal support, possibly including counselling. This needs sensitive handling; telling them that that this problem is a marvellous opportunity, whilst quite possibly true, may not be particularly helpful.

Drifting

The stuck people have no lack of consciousness; if anything, they think too much and do too little about their situation. The second pattern is in this respect the opposite; in it, people move rapidly and frequently between jobs, organizations, communities, countries and professions. Initial enthusiasm for each situation is quickly followed by disappointment or boredom.

The incidence of this drifting lifestyle among highly-educated, articulate people since the sixties has been one of the most significant social phenomena of recent decades. It is an expression of the epidemic crisis of commitment — that is, the inability to make and sustain commitment — which has characterized a whole generation in western society. We see it perhaps most clearly in the field of relationships, where the promiscuity of youth is often followed by what has become known as "serial monogamy" — a succession of partnerships lasting anything from a few months to several decades; what seems permanent today may prove otherwise, sooner or later.

Drifters, by definition, lack a sense of direction. They "follow their feet," which often lead them into a rich variety of social, personal and work experiences. This can become an addictive pattern; however, it also, sooner or later, becomes unsatisfying. The longing to find the "real thing" grows as the energy of youth dwindles. Variety and change no longer compensate for a lack of depth. The need to build a longer-term commitment to a single professional field becomes increasingly urgent from the late twenties onward; if not satisfied, it can take on existential proportions a decade later. "Here I am, nearly forty, and I still haven't *really become anything* ..."

Drifting is movement without consciousness. Overcoming this means starting to make much more thoroughly considered choices. Choosing *for* something is easy for drifters; but every choice to take a particular direction is simultaneously a decision *not* to pursue other options, at least for the time being, perhaps not ever. This is what is so hard; to specialize, to say "No" to other possibilities, is painful for these people.

Sometimes, the "real thing" image has to be abandoned altogether. The ideal, commitment–inspiring vocation may never materialize. What is essential, though, is for ex–drifters to clarify and formulate their own central *values,* and to apply these faithfully via whatever skills they can learn or have acquired, in a longer–term work role. These values are the basis for commitment. The "longer–term" is important not only for pragmatic reasons, but also to provide a context in which individuals can experience the consequences and the fruits of their own efforts.

Feeling our way forward

Many variations on these themes of drifting and stuckness can be observed — the dreamer who is outwardly stuck and inwardly drifting; the obsessive who is inwardly stuck and can never find the outer situation to match his fixed mental picture; the escapist who runs from all self–confrontation, inner or outer; and so on.

What is needed is *a sense of conscious movement.* Neither thought nor will alone, or even in combination, can create this. The clarity of thinking must not be squandered in endless analysis; it must be used to formulate and explore meaningful questions, to create living pictures of past, present and possible futures, and to test the reality of aspirations, resources and potential. The energy of will must not be dissipated in impulsiveness or self–pressurizing; it must engage in a disciplined process of inner and outer initiative, so that destiny can become visible "out of the movement." The orientation and integration for both thought and will must arise from the feeling life — not as in "feeling sorry for oneself," but as in "feeling one's way." Only the heart can judge which impulses are creative, which images should become reality.

"Job" as mirage

The discussion so far has been about the struggle of individuals to find their way towards meaningful work. These personal dramas, however, are today played out in a societal context which is itself undergoing a far–reaching upheaval. There is increasing evidence that the way in which work is organized in society is changing fundamentally and permanently. We are entering the post–employment era.

The most cogent and convincing prophet of this change in Britain is Charles Handy, Visiting Professor at the London Business School. In his books *The Future of Work* and more recently *The Age of Unreason,* he argues that "discontinuous change" now faces society, and will require "new ways of thinking about jobs, careers, remuneration, and the whole shape of our lives." Specifically, he present a well–researched picture of an emerging work–culture in which long–term employment within an organization is less and less the norm. When his own children left college he told them: "I hope you won't go looking for a job." What he meant was that "rather than scurrying about looking for a corporate ladder to climb or a professional trajectory to follow, they ought to develop a product, skill, or service, assemble a portfolio that illustrates these assets and then go out and find customers."

In "threefold" terms, the job is a "rights" relationship between employer (organization) and employee (individual) which is supposed to allow us to "find our place" at work. It has to connect the "cultural" striving of the individual towards self–realization, with the "economic" function of satisfying the needs of others through work. Ideally, it should provide us with daily tasks which contribute to the aims of the organiza- tion whilst at the same time allowing us to fulfil our unique personal mission on the earth.

This is an enormous gulf to span, and of course few jobs ever achieve this. Why should we have ever imagined that an arrangement as banal as employment could do so?

Reliance on the "job" — meaning full–time organizational employment — as a way of finding one's place, will become more and more futile. Already, less than half of all adults of working age are in this "normal" situation. The rest are self- employed, part–time or temporary workers or unemployed. The age of employment was a relatively brief one in human history — a couple of centuries or so — and will soon be a thing of the past, at least as far as most people are concerned.

Where does its passing leave us? At worst, with an increas- ingly fragmented, divided and chaotic society, in which iso- lated individuals, driven and insecure, scrabble and compete for scraps of work and money. At best, with clearer and wider choices, more transparent economic relationships, and the flexibility to compose the style of living and working which individually suits us. Handy describes the increase of "port- folio people" who mix different kinds of work — some done for money, some for interest or out of social responsibility — with the needs of their domestic situations and their own development.

* * *

Finding one's place — or places — in post–employment society poses yet another tremendous challenge to human development. It requires on the one hand, a deepening and strengthening of personal identity and self–responsibility; and on the other, the development of social and organizational forms which can recreate a degree of wholeness in each work situation.

Personal integration: vocation as inner orientation

The new realities, both individual and social, which we are now experiencing, will require a new understanding of concepts such as *career, vocation* and *profession.* These represent levels of reality which each person needs to discover and develop in themselves through their working life.

At the highest level, we may hope gradually to develop a certain intuitive sense of our own deepest purpose in life — of the intentions, responsibilities and undertakings prepared before birth and crystallized by the encounters into which destiny leads us. A greater or lesser part of this personal mission may express itself through what we usually call "work." At this level, the work involved in our own inner development, and the work involved in our private relationships, may be just as significant as our external career.

For many people, however, the impulse will arise sooner or later to express aspects of this individual mission through work which addresses a particular area of human need. *Vocation,* in this sense, is a breathing–in or inspiration of the suffering and incompleteness of humanity: it is recognizing the "calling" to contribute to the fulfilment of something unfinished in the world. It takes us beyond our individual karma and connects us to a broad stream of human development such as education, art, healing, human rights, agriculture or the production of economic goods or services.

Whereas vocation is a set of values and purposes which "speak" to us, *profession* is what we speak or represent to others. What we "profess to be" is an image of a particular *community of workers* in a specific field. Each profession has its own mental picture of itself as a worldwide grouping with common aims and interests. By identifying with a profession, I connect myself implicitly or explicitly with certain collective ethics and standards, and I can receive the benefit of the accumulated and developing expertise of others within my field, as well as (often) various types of professional associations which try to represent and uphold the image and status of the profession.

On these three levels, then, we can "find our place" as a personal reality, independently of any concrete work situation:

> *Mission* — unique individual purpose;
>
> *Vocation* — commitment to a realm of universal human need;
>
> *Profession* — participation in shared self-image of collegial community.

Employment connects these three with a specific context via the job or position to which one is appointed: through an organizational arrangement, Mission, Vocation and Profession "incarnate" — into what?

Social integration — "Whole work"

Managers of organizations and projects are responsible, among other things, for creating and developing structures and arrangements which form the framework for others' work. These include physical structures such as workplace layout and technology, process structures such as job design and information systems, and social structures such as departmental responsibilities, work group composition and remuneration. Just as the architecture of a building can support or inhibit the activities which take place within it, or a person's physical body can enable or hinder the self-expression of the incarnating individuality, so these "work structures" can nurture or deform the working lives of those who must inhabit them.

In Steiner's day, the progressive division of labour was increasingly destroying the "wholeness" of work, fragmenting it into smaller and smaller repetitive tasks, and thereby robbing the worker of meaning and satisfaction. This deformation of work has been a continuing and world-wide process; but now, in this time of "discontinuous change," some new principles for the organization of work are struggling to emerge.

Enlightened managers now perceive that beyond a certain point, the further division of labour and reduction of workers to "hands" becomes counter-productive and wasteful. In particular, it is wasteful of human capacities. In the most advanced organizations, the involvement and empowerment of grass-roots workers is now a priority. Creativity, responsibility and participation in constant innovation — for long regarded as the province of management alone — are now increasingly required from everyone. Through movements such as "Total Quality" and "Employee Involvement," opportunities are emerging to create more healthy and "whole" work situations. What will this involve?

Firstly, each worker and work group must be allocated a "whole task" — that is, a process or step in a process which has a degree of completeness to it; in which significant value is created; and which can be planned, carried out and evaluated as far as possible by the workers themselves. These conditions allow a sense of ownership and responsibility to be developed.

Secondly, the focus of this responsibility must shift from the boss to the *customer*. Customers may be external consumers of the product or service, or internal to the organization itself (for instance, the next work group in the production process). Instead of only asking "What does my manager want?" workers must increasingly ask "Who is my customer, and what does he/she need from me?" In this question, something of the underlying fraternal principle of economic life is revealed: on a lower level, it echoes the biblical "Who is my neighbour?" It is significant that when receiving a service, we can intuitively tell the difference between someone who is *genuinely* interested in our needs, and someone who has merely been trained to *appear to be so*. (This has far–reaching implications; it potentially re–aligns morality with organizational success — though there are of course also many factors tending in the opposite direction.)

Thirdly, meaningful *participation* must be available to every co–worker, in the common aims and concerns of the work-community. The cultivation and guidance of frank and productive *meetings* is essential in this. Increasingly, the role of leaders and managers will be as "conductors of the orchestra" in these participative work cultures.

The "whole work situation," then, must "offer a place" to individuals on these three levels:

Participation — co–responsibility;

Processes — customer orientation, service;

Tasks — completeness, value creation, ownership.

Three future challenges

A healthy society would be one in which "whole people" do "whole work" — where the self–actualizing principle of a free cultural life feeds, and is fed by, the mutuality principle of economics. It is the task of the rights life — arrangements, agreements, contracts — to bring these two into a creative relationship, and so enable individuals to "find their place." Employment is only one possible form of such arrangements. We need to discover and develop many more; forms based on mutual respect, fairness and central human values. (This would be a subject for another article!) They will be contracts *for* service, not contracts *of* service. Most of us will need to negotiate a series of these throughout our working lives, to recreate continually the connection between our personal sense of mission, vocation and professional identity, and the responsibilities, processes and concrete tasks which await us in each successive work context.

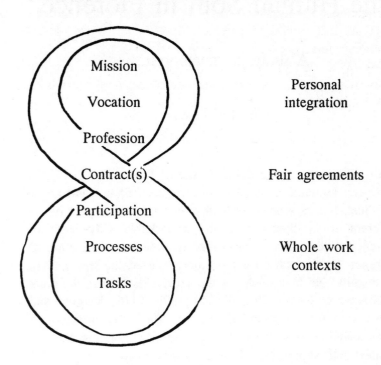

Mission	Personal
Vocation	integration
Profession	
Contract(s)	Fair agreements
Participation	
Processes	Whole work
Tasks	contexts

Acknowledgements
For many of the ideas in this article I am indebted to my colleagues, especially Ernst Amons and George Perry of the Centre for Social Development at Emerson College, and Christian Schumacher, originator of the "whole work" concept.

The Flowering of the Human Soul in Florence

A study in metamorphosis

Charles Lawrie

With the advent of the cultural Age of Pisces in c.1415 AD, European humanity experienced a mighty call to stand on its own feet. Spirits who were to demonstrate this imperative in different ways clustered to the remarkable City–State of Florence. Even today, we can discern how the architecture of Florence set the stage for the emergence of the free human personality. No feature shows this more clearly than the great Cupola which Filippo Brunelleschi (1379–1446) designed and constructed for the cathedral of Santa Maria dei Fiori, which focuses and warms the skyline of the city. For this was the greatest self–supporting dome in human history.

The five–hour ceremony of its consecration on 25 March 1436 fulfilled the Florentine sense for colourful procession magnificently. Pope Eugene IV was in residence at Santa Maria Novella, where Dante had once imbibed the doctrine of Thomas Aquinas. Christopher Hibbert wrote:

> A wooden walk, raised on stilts, hung with banners
> and garlands and covered by a scarlet canopy, was
> constructed between the Pope's apartments and the
> door of the Cathedral. At the appointed hour the Pope
> appeared, clothed in white and wearing his jewelled
> tiara, and began the slow procession along the carpet

which had been laid over the raised boards beneath the canopy. He was followed by seven cardinals, by thirty-seven bishops and archbishops, and by the leading officials of the City, led by the Gonfaloniere [the standard-bearer of the Republic, whose banner showed a red lily on a white ground — hence the Cathedral name: Maria dei Fiori] and the Priori, [whose crimson coats lined with ermine betokened their high office]. At the sound of the choir singing their hymn of praise many of the spectators were seen to be in tears.

The rise of the Medicis

Florence was recovering her soul after a period of ordeal. For in September 1433, one month before the birth in nearby Figline of Marsilio Ficino, she had suffered a contest among her leading citizens between the haughty soldier-diplomat, Rinaldo degli Albizzi, and the sober and cultured merchant-banker, Cosimo de Medici (1389–1464). Their conflict derived from the popular response to the fiasco of the Albizzi-led war on Lucca; but it concerned effective power in the Republic. Cosimo was sent into exile — though when, on Michaelmas Day 1433, the *Capitano del Popolo* entered his little cell in the bell-tower of the Palazzo Vecchio to inform him of his sentence, Cosimo was prepared for death.

Within a year, public discontent ousted the Albizzis, and on September 28, 1434, one day after his forty-fifth birthday, Cosimo set out for Florence from Venice, with an escort of three hundred. Wrote Machiavelli:

Seldom has a citizen returning from a great victory been greeted by such a concourse of people and with such demonstrations of affection as Cosimo on his return from exile. [But from now on, he could not merely] live powerfully and safely in Florence like everyone else.

Cosimo was obliged to work more deliberately to secure support in the elections of the State.

Medici popularity had ripened ever since June 1378 when Gonfaloniere Salvestro de Medici effectively led "the earliest of all proletarian insurrections" (S. Weil) — the revolt of the *Ciompi* — and established Medici solidarity with the downtrodden members of the *minuto popolo,* particularly the woolcarders. But it was Giovanni de Medici (1360–1429), of another branch of the family, and Cosimo's father, who established the Medici role in the Florentine State. Goethe described him as almost a saint, who united benevolence and business sense in like measure. As a member of both the wool–working and banking guilds, by his efforts, the Medicis steadily became the chief bankers of Europe, following the demise of the Knights Templar. From his leading role in the bankers' guild, Giovanni helped to supply capital and connections for enterprises of the Florentine State. He conducted business in sixteen European capitals, including Geneva, London and Bruges. He became banker to the Papal Curia, and his twenty–five–year old son Cosimo accompanied Pope John XXIII as financial adviser to the Council of Constance in 1414. The *fiorino d'oro,* the golden florin of Florence was used and respected throughout Europe. The terms of Florentine banking entered banking vocabulary world–wide (for instance, *banco, cassa, credito, debito*). At home, Giovanni supported tax reforms which benefitted the poor, and not the rich. When he died in 1429, as Machiavelli observed: "he was rich in property, but richer in the respect and love of the people."

Question of interest

A particular moral dilemma faced Christian bankers then emerging from the medieval perspective: how should they amend for charging interest on their loans, a practice which was still felt to be immoral? The Church shrewdly advised the bankers to compensate to the same amount before their death.

Now a man appeared who was to give the equivalent of over
£20 million to the cultural and architectural improvement of
Florence between 1429 and 1464. The flowering of the
Florentine Renaissance would be unthinkable without this
stream of intuitively–guided gift–money at its root. But it
would also be inconceivable without his and his son's and
grandson's influence in the conduct of state, and without the
particular enlightened quality of their culture.

Cosimo united the benevolence and acumen of his father,
with a rich humanist culture. He was a genuine striving soul.
The context of his culture was at first, the classical *Latin*
humanism of Petrarch, represented by the Chancellor of Florence, Coluccio Salutati (1331–1406), but it came to include
influence from the *Greek*. In 1397, Salutati invited the Byzantine scholar Manuel Chrysoloras to become the first Professor
of Greek at Florence University. Chrysoloras encouraged his
pupils, among them Roberto de Rossi, to find and translate the
rest of Plato's dialogues from the Greek. Cosimo learned
Greek from de Rossi, and his interest was sufficient to send
him on a bibliophile expedition with his friend Poggo Bra-
cciolini in search of classical Greek and Latin manuscripts
among the monasteries of the North.

The council to reunite the Church

World–events were beating around Florence. With the Otto-
man Turks threatening his Byzantine Empire, John VII Paleologus, and Patriarch Joseph of the Eastern Orthodox Church,
were impelled to seek to reunify Christendom, and win
powerful Western support. Pope Eugene IV was particularly
responsive, since the credit for such reunion would immeasur-
ably strengthen his own position *vis–à–vis* the dissident
Council of Basel. Hence the leaders of the Greek and Latin
Churches agreed to convene in General Council at Ferrara in
1438. But when plague struck Ferrara in the winter of that
year, Cosimo de Medici stepped in.

He invited the Council to move further south, to Florence. Since Pope Eugene was his friend and a resident of Florence, and since Cosimo offered free accommodation in plenty and a loan of 1500 florins per month so long as the Council remained in session, his invitation was accepted. The Council moved to Florence, and on February 26, 1439, the Chancellor of Florence, Leonardo Bruni (1369–1444), welcomed the delegates with a fluent speech in Greek.

This was the moment at which a world–historic process began in earnest. In the words of Rudolf Steiner (Berlin, Nov 13, 1911): "The Age of Greece — which was a kind of centre among the seven Post–Atlantean epochs — underwent a certain renewal in the Renaissance." Benozzo Gozzoli has conveyed the ethos of this renewal with radiant imagination in his frescoes for the walls of the Chapel of the Palazzo Medici built for Cosimo by his friend Michelozzo between 1444 and 1452. (He began them in 1459). Here we behold the three Kings, wearing gold crowns, leading their respective companies on horseback or mule towards the distant Mother and Child (original by Lippi). Who are these resplendent figures? — The Byzantine Emperor John Paleologus, the Orthodox Patriarch Joseph, and the young grandson of Cosimo, Lorenzo de Medici (1449–92)!

Amongst the company who follow the Golden King, Lorenzo, behind the youthful figure of Marsilio Ficino, we see the bearded countenances of some venerable Greeks — and it was one such who was now profoundly to influence Cosimo de Medici and the spirit of the Florentine Renaissance.

Plethon and Greek philosophy

George Gemistos (known also as Plethon) had travelled to the General Council from Greece in the same papal ship as the legate, Nicholas of Cusa. During the voyage, the latter received the night–inspiration for his *De Docta Ignorantia* which he composed in 1439–40. A profoundly schooled philosophic reason, a deep philosophical earnest, radiate from Plethon's spirit. One may meditate on the lapidary power of his reply to the lengthy criticism of Scholarios concerning Plethon's account of the differences between Plato and Aristotle:

> Philosophy consists in a few words on a few subjects: it is about the principles of being which, if a man has thoroughly grasped them, enable him to discern accurately everything else that can come to men's knowledge.

Plethon stood in an initiate tradition. He considered that Plato's philosophy had come down via the Pythagoreans from Zoroaster in c. 6000 BC. According to Paul Oskar Kristeller, he was apparently the first to attribute *The Chaldaic Oracles* to Zoroaster, and he wrote a commentary on these which Ficino was later to translate. Following Proclus and Psellos, he considered not only Zoroaster, but also Hermes, Orpheus and Pythagoras as exponents of the mystery–wisdom which Plato re–expressed, views which undoubtedly influenced Cosimo and Ficino. But how did this influence come about?

Plethon attended the General Council as one of three lay advisers to the Greek delegation, with two of his pupils, the Metropolitans of Nicaea and Ephesus, Ioannos Bessarion and Mark Eugenikos. They were asked to advise on the order of topics to be discussed. With exemplary penetration, Plethon and Eugenikos insisted on dealing with the *Filioque* first, as its credal inclusion had been "the cause and origin of the Schism." Plethon drew up a draft concerning the related question of the Procession of the Holy Spirit, on which the whole 'Reunion' was eventually to turn. But the eighty–year-old philosopher was impartial to the specific course of the consultations. Bessarion could stand in for him. Instead, he found that the Florentine humanists desired to hear from him all that he could tell them, for instance, concerning the differences between Plato and Aristotle. One such difference concerned the burning question of the immortality of the human soul.

With this question I believe we approach the core of the
Platonic element in the Florentine Renaissance. For it is con-
ceivable that Cosimo's expectation of the death sentence in
September 1433 deepened his whole relation to this question,
so that Plethon's demonstration of the immortality of the
human soul according to Plato affected him with particular
force. Even as he lay dying at Careggi in 1464, he was listening to Ficino reading from Plato's pupil, Xenocrates, concerning death and the immortality of the human soul. Furthermore,
we may recognize in Ficino's own asking and answering of
this question, which in Kristeller's view came to "occupy a
more important place in his system than ... in the thought of
any other thinker before or after him," elements of the con-
stancy of Cosimo's striving for cognition in this matter, both
before and even after his death.

> The political regime founded by Cosimo de Medici
> and perfected by his grandson Lorenzo, [wrote Curt
> Gutkind] differed from the despotic states of
> fifteenth–century Italy in the preservation of
> republican institutions [which protected the freedom
> of the citizens, their equality before the law and their
> equal right to office (Bruni)]. Even its critics had to
> admit that the Medici acted within ... the constitution.

This approach derived from their ability to perceive the souls
of their fellow–citizens. But this ability flowered to the full in
a free cultural institution which came to ray its soul throughout Europe, and which centred in the soul of Marsilio Ficino
(1433–99).

The Academy

Writing in the Preface to his translation of Plotinus in 1492
(a work which Pico della Mirandola had encouraged him to
undertake), Ficino recalled:

> At the time when the Council was in progress
> between the Greeks and the Latins at Florence under

Pope Eugenius, the great Cosimo, whom a decree of
the Signoria designated *Pater Patriae,* often listened
to the Greek philosopher Gemistos (with the
cognomen Plethon, as it were a second Plato) while
he expounded the mysteries of Platonism. And he
was so immediately inspired, so moved by Gemistos'
fervent tongue, that as a result he conceived in his
noble mind a kind of *Academy,* which he was to
bring to birth at the first opportune moment. Later,
when the great Medici brought his great idea into
being, he destined me, the son of his favourite doctor,
while I was still a boy, for the task.

A letter from Ficino to Cosimo on September 4, 1462
contains the first mention of the Academy, but a letter from
Cosimo to Ficino in that year reveals its spirit:

Yesterday I went to my estate at Careggi, but for the
sake of cultivating my mind and not the estate. Come
to us, Marsilio, as soon as possible. Bring with you
Plato's book on the Highest Good [Philebus], which I
suppose you have translated from Greek into Latin as
you promised. I want nothing more wholeheartedly
than to know which way leads most surely to happiness. Farewell. Come, and bring your Orphic lyre
with you.

Let us allow motifs from this letter to blossom within us.
Cultivating ... the estate. Cosimo loved country life, and
used to wander in the lands of his villa at Careggi, pruning his
vines and tending his olives, planting mulberries and pink-
flowering almond–trees. Some way uphill from his villa, at
Montevecchio in 1462, he settled Ficino in a little farm, which
became the home of the Florentine Platonic Academy. But
Villa Careggi drew the Academicians to its rooms and flowering gardens, modelled on the olive–grove of Akademe near
Athens, where Plato lived and taught for fifty years. Here,
along its sheltered walks, and by its statues, pools and foun-
tains, we should imagine these jovial spirits, in friendly and

earnest conversation. And it was here, on the initiative of nineteen-year-old Lorenzo de Medici, that friends of the Academy assembled for the first time in twelve hundred years on November 7, 1468, to celebrate the birth and death of Plato, by reading and discoursing on his *Symposium,* his colloquy on Love.

Bring Plato's book ... which I suppose you have translated. With the farm-villa, Cosimo gave Ficino a number of Greek manuscripts to translate. In five years, he translated the entire works of Plato, as well as the *Corpus Hermeticum.* Then, following the *Convivio* of 1468, he composed his *De Amore,* and in 1469 he began his eighteen-volume *Platonic Theology, on the Immortality of Souls,* which was printed in 1482. This work drew Pico della Mirandola to his side in 1484.

I want nothing more wholeheartedly than to know which way leads most surely to happiness. Two years before his death, Cosimo was still striving for the Highest Good, in the company of Ficino and Plato. Following Plato's educational ideal, he ensured that leading Academicians, including Landino, Becchi, Argyropolou, and above all, Ficino, became tutors to his grandson, Lorenzo.

Come, and bring your Orphic lyre with you. Ficino was an inspired musician. He wrote once to the German astronomer Paulus Middelburgensis:

> Our century, like a golden age, restored to light the
> liberal arts that were nearly extinct — grammar,
> poetry, rhetoric, painting, sculpture, architecture,
> music, the ancient performance of songs with the
> Orphic lyre, and all that in Florence ... And in
> Florence it restored the Platonic doctrine from
> darkness to light.

To Martinus Uranius, he wrote that his friends and pupils were "not drawn together by any kind of social intercourse or comradeship, but by a *communion in the liberal arts.*" Music was a means of this communion. Once, when his companions sank into despair at the Turkish advance in the East, Ficino took his lyre and by his playing alone, fired them with new courage. When Lorenzo first heard Ficino playing his lyre, he "thought that Orpheus was returning to the world" About 1484, Ficino penned *De Rationibus Musicae* following Plato, Trismegistus and Pythagoras, in which he discussed the proportions underlying the intervals, acknowledged the soft harmony of the third, and compared the third, fifth and octave to the Three Graces!

One can scarcely exaggerate the musical ethos of the cultural interplay which was to spring to life in Florence with the accession of Lorenzo de Medici in 1469, at the age of twenty. Like his mother Lucrezia, he was a gifted poet. The dancing measures of the Tuscan vernacular, the wellspring of the new Italian language, played upon his lips. He sang his songs in the streets.

Friends of genius responded, two of whom he had drawn into his own house: Agnolo Poliziano (1454–94) and Sandro Botticelli (1445–1510). In early Spring 1475, all Florence thrilled to a Tournament (Giostra) for Lorenzo's younger brother, Giuliano. Everyone knew that Giuliano was really in love with the beautiful wife of Marco Vespucci, Simonetta Cattaneo. Simonetta was led to the Throne of the *Queen of Beauty*.

Giuliano appeared before her, wearing her favour,
and with a standard by Botticelli depicting Pallas
Athene, goddess of wisdom and war, looking upon
Cupid who stood bound to the bole of an olive-tree
with his bow and broken arrow at his feet. [Hibbert].

Botticelli's Primavera

Now Poliziano composed his *Stanze cominciate per la Giostra di Giuliano de Medici* (1475–78), which established him as the finest Italian poet of his century. With laughing heart, and in sparkling octaves, he painted imaginations of a young "Iulio" being gently awoken by Cupid and a beautiful nymph named Simonetta, to Love and the eternal Garden of Venus. The being of this planetary sphere, in its highest as well as its intermediary nature, pours to us in musical poetry from Poliziano, and it inspired Botticelli to create his musical *Primavera*.

No picture in Florence today conveys to us more immediately the ethos of the Florentine Platonic Academy than this painting by Botticelli, created in 1477–78 for the young cousins of Lorenzo de Medici, and now in the Galleria Uffizi. (Some say that Ficino advised in its composition.) It breathes the full radiance of the fragrant flower, before its petals wither, and the essence flows into the seed. We may note the flame–tipped arrow of the hovering blind–fold Cupid, which portrays the fiery will to incarnation of the unborn soul, drawing its parents together on earth in the community of love. His arrow aims at the heart of the Grace of Willing, whose gaze rests on the lively countenance of Mercury, dispelling the vapours that wreathe about the fruiting apricots with his winged caduceus. Following Ovid and Poliziano, the metamorphoses of Love are indicated in the three Mothers to the right: in the nymph Chloris, whom Zephyr chases with amorous haste; in Flora, the real Primavera, who flings forth roses from her lap of plenty; and in the hierophant of the whole episode, chaste Venus, who looks at us in unquestioning beauty from the centre of the etheric universe with comprehending gaze, and whose gesturing palm conducts the melody of the entire sequence. The radiant aura of the morning–star shines about her. The whole picture is a drama of musical metamorphosis. The chords descend and ascend through the stirring influence of the males upon the responsive plenipotentials of the females. What is the secret meaning of this sequence of evolution from Venus to Mercury?

But we must end. We cannot now follow the fortunes and misfortunes of Lorenzo: the death of Simonetta; the murder of his brother; his own narrow escape from death; the gradual demise of the Medici bank, and the onset of his illness. He was no banker, but a poet, an inspired statesman, a patron unrivalled in history. Michelangelo, Leonardo owed their early nurture to him. He presided in Florence, and indeed Italy, at a time when, following the great wave of Aristotle which flowed into twelfth and thirteenth century Europe from the Arabs, the wave of Plato flowed in fourteenth and fifteenth century complement from the Greeks. For these were the twin foci of the metamorphosing School of Sophia, revealed in fullness by Raphael in his Stanze. Anthropos–Sophia was not yet born in the Age of Pisces, but she was coming.

The Turks took Byzantium. The Byzantines stepped back, as Pope Eugene had foreseen, from their brief reunion with the Roman Church. New powers began to dominate from the North. New worlds were emerging in the West. On the day when Pico della Mirandola, the last blazing flame of the Florentine Platonic Academy, died on November 17, 1494, the troops of the French king marched into Florence, and sacked the Medici Villa at Careggi. Lorenzo, Poliziano, had gone before him, two years, and two months before. So fell the seed. But it can spring to life again in every heart which desires to heed the true secret of Venus. This secret speaks to us from the mouth of the Man with the Lamp at the culmination of Goethe's alchemical *Tale of the Green Snake and the Beautiful Lily* (1795):

Die Liebe herrscht nicht, aber sie bildet, und das ist mehr.
Love does not rule, it educates, and that is more.

Select bibliography:
Christopher Hibbert, *The Rise and Fall of the House of Medici,* Penguin 1974.
Paul Oskar Kristeller, *The Philosophy of Marsilio Ficino,* Columbia 1943.
Curt Gutkind, *Cosimo de Medici,* Oxford 1938.
C.M. Woodhouse, *George Gemistos Plethon,* Oxford 1986.

Review

Paul Law

Andrew Welburn, *The Book with Fourteen Seals*,
Rudolf Steiner Press, 1992, £20.95

The Book with Fourteen Seals is the title of Andrew Welburn's
new study of the *Apocalypse of Adam*. The original, which is
available in several translations, comes form the Coptic
Gnostic library discovered at Nag Hammadi in 1945. It
belongs to the "apocalypse" literature that was common in
Jewish writings between 200 BC and 200 AD, but which is
likely to pose difficulties for the reader unfamiliar with the
genre. "Pseudoepigraphia" (or "false writings") of this kind
claim to have been written by much earlier Biblical authors:
they appear to narrate history from a much earlier age, under
the guise of prophecy — and to exploit the credibility thereby
gained to win credence for their own prophetic utterances.
Andrew Welburn proposes a radically alternative view of these
writings: he argues that to dismiss the genre as a species of
forgery is entirely to miss the point. Originality and authenti-
city are *modern,* post renaissance literary criteria: they proceed
from a sense of self, of authorship, that was unknown even in
Chaucer's age. Far from deceiving his readers, the writer of
pseudoepigraphy was offering them something far more auth-
entic than he, from his restricted viewpoint in the present,
could hope to offer. Instead, he would immerse himself so
thoroughly in the past that he could draw upon the memory of

past figures: he could momentarily *become* Enoch or Ezra or Adam, and speak with their voice.

Such is the case with the *Apocalypse of Adam*. It purports to be a prophetic revelation from the dying Adam to his son, Seth. From internal evidence, the text can be dated to the early part of the first century BC: the author was probably a member of an Essene community in Syria, (perhaps even a follower of the Christian Gnostic Valentinus). Even allowing for a familiarity with the genre, the *Apocalypse* is not an inviting book — a chiaroscuro of brilliant impenetrable images, resonant but tantalizingly obscure. But it has deservedly attracted scholarly attention since Alexander Bohlig in the sixties pointed out the confluence of Iranian and Jewish elements that underlie it.

Unlike most other works found at Nag Hammadi the *Apocalypse* points to those preparations for the Christ event that were rooted in the mystery traditions of the East, particularly the teachings of Zoroastrianism. Andrew Welburn advances the thesis that the "seals" which form the core of the book are each precisely encoded accounts of the incarnations of Zarathustra: twelve of those incarnations had become historical fact when the *Apocalypse* was composed — probably by an Essene author early in the first century BC The thirteenth incarnation was earnestly awaited.

Readers of Andrew Welburn's previous book — *The Beginnings of Christianity* — will already be familiar with his exposition of the *Apocalypse* as evidence of the reception of Iranian spirituality by Jewish Essene communities. What emerged from this encounter was not a mere revival of ancient initiation wisdom, but a transformation of that wisdom in the real of ethical individuality — an anticipation of the new relationship of the human and the divine achieved by Christianity. In the present work, however, the focus is on the *Apocalypse* itself and the role of Zarathustra — the Illuminator — in preparing mankind for the advent of Christ.

The author proceeds by treating each "seal" in turn as a riddle that will yield its meaning only when the appropriate mythic terms and context are recognized. The difficulty in such "decoding" exercises is that the original material is essentially a composition of images: to interpret them with confidence requires a daunting combination of imaginative responsiveness and critical discernment. This is a combination that Andrew Welburn demonstrates strongly in the present work.

We can "solve" a riddle, a mystery, a "seal" in two quite different senses. We can "explain" it in such a way that the unknown terms are identified, the mystery is solved, the right answer is found. In such a case, our interest ceases as soon as the explanation is completed. On the other, there is the sort of explanation that clarifies and illuminates, and that leaves us with more to contemplate at the end of the explanation than at the beginning: the mystery grows more mysterious; it suggests further connections, other secrets yet to be unravelled. This is the case with Andrew Welburn's reading of *The Apocalypse of Adam:* he does not only offer a convincing identification of the successive incarnations of Zarathustra — he also gives a picture of how each incarnation contributed to human evolution, and of how the incarnations culminated in the birth of Jesus and the visitation of the Magi.

Thus we can see a broad pattern within the first twelve incarnations, by breaking them down into cycles of three. In the first (Andrew Welburn calls this the "Cycle of Zarathustra), the great teachings of Ohrmazd and Ahriman, the opposition of light and Darkness, was expounded and linked to man's task of transforming nature. In the second cycle (the "Cycle of Ushedar") the Illuminator was concerned with the purging of the Semitic cultures in preparation for their vital role in post–Atlantean evolution. In the third (the "Cycle of Ushedarmah) he brought together the wisdom of Babylonian science with the Iranian Mysteries of Light and the emerging rationalism of Greece, thereby preparing the way for the replacement of the old mythological consciousness of mankind. In the final cycle (the "Cycle of Soshyans") his initiation in Egyptian Hermeticism led to the revelation of the human archetype that had been obscured since the Fall, and the coming transformation of the man in the advent of Christ. In the final incarnation of this fourth cycle, the Illuminator is concerned to introduce the prophetic knowledge of Jewish esotericism — perhaps of the Essenes — into the Egyptian Mysteries.

Perhaps the most impressive element of this book. however, is its visionary closing chapter: "On Mount Hukhairya." Here we join the Zoroastrian Magi in their periodic pilgrimages to the holy mountain of Charaxio/Hukhaurya, where they consulted a book of revelation — perhaps a book of images not unlike *The Apocalypse of Adam* itself — by which they were able to trace the twelve successive incarnations of the Illuminator as they were reflected in rhythms of the zodiac. Whereas the zodiacal qualities of the incarnations would have been known to Magian priests, it was Jewish esotericism that added the concept of an "apocalyptic" thirteenth incarnation — in Zoroastrian terms the awesome thought of the incarnation of the pure Light itself.

Letter

Dear Editor,

I have just been reading your article "Language & Nationhood" in the 1992 *Golden Blade* and am most intrigued with it.

There are many questions I should like to ask but I'd have to do some research first; I am really writing to elaborate on your touch of New Zealandese!

I'm struck by the fact that the words you quote in American are, I think, truly in common use and would be found in an American dictionary whereas I can't help feeling that the Australian and "Kiwi" words are at best recent slang which one finds passing through any language and dying off after a while and only to be scoffed at later as very old hat. The Ausie words certainly speak of our lazy speech down here — prezzy is certainly current over here though I haven't heard the others.

Now — to come to ours! I think someone may be pulling your leg! The phrase is "rattle your dags!" and would be used only in farming circles I should think. I'd doubt you'd ever hear it in the city! You'd apply it to someone in a light hearted way — someone who was shilly shallying — say a child dragging behind on a walk. You might say "Come on, get a move on, rattle your dags."

To explain this: When a sheep is heavy with wool and hasn't been shorn recently and pasture has suddenly become lush, the effect on the sheep is the same as someone eating too many figs. The sloshy stools stick to the wool near the anus forming festoons of dried faeces on the sheep's rear. These can become quite thick and when the poor creature moves from a walk to a run they rattle like so many hanging beads." Usually in this situation the flock is "crutched" which means that the wool round the sheep's backsides is shorn off. This is certainly done before lambing or shearing.

I've certainly never heard anyone claiming to rattle their own dags! and as your can imagine it's not likely to be in common usage.

   Sincerely
     Patricia Ojala (Mrs)

Notes about the authors

Dorit Winter is the director of the San Francisco Extension Programme of the Rudolf Steiner College Teacher Training Course.

Christopher Marcus was born in Edinburgh in 1950. He was a pupil at Elmfield Steiner School, completed a training at the Drama Centre, London, graduated from the Speech and Drama School in Dornach, and now has his own drama company, *Theatre of the World* recently renamed, *September Theatre* in Holland.

Charles Lawrie, writer and poet, was born in Scotland in 1947, grew up in Wales, and is currently editor of *Shoreline,* a journal for the working spirit.

Steve Briault is a consultant in the field of organizational and management development. Previously he has worked in the Camphill movement in refugee settlement and as a school administrator. For five years he was a staff member at the Centre for Social Development, Emerson College, where he continues to teach on a regular visiting basis. He lives in the Hoathly Hill community in Sussex.

Tobias

School of Art A three-year training is offered
based on Goethe's theory of colour
and Rudolf Steiner's colour dynamics

Artistic Therapy

Artistic Therapy is a new approach to the whole human being to be seen distinctly as a synthesizing approach rather than analytical or diagnostic. Taking place on the soul level, creative forces of the individuality are activated which then are able to act upon the deeper-lying bodily processes.

Painting as a therapy begins with the cultivation of healthy breathing. This extends to the painting process itself as regards rhythm and colour relationships. Such an approach will strengthen the warmth constitution and help patients overcoming fear.

Art works through the human being's threefold nature: the life of intellect, feeling and will. In particular, the middle realm, the feeling life, needs recognition and strengthening in times when there is a tendency of an over-intellectual development from childhood onward.

For healing it is necessary for the patient to develop inner activity through the artistic processes. This can be a positive gesture towards the future, base on an awareness of the spiritual needs of our time.

For full details write or telephone to
TOBIAS SCHOOL OF ART
Coombe Hill Road, East Grinstead, Sussex RH19 4LZ
Tel. 0342-313655 & 314 515

Thirteen to Nineteen: Discovering the Light

Conversations with parents

Julian Sleigh

Adolescence creeps quietly into the life of a child bringing many changes and much inner conflict. The author sheds light on the familiar problems of loneliness, meeting with others and relating to them, difficulties with parents, awakening of sexuality, drink and drugs.

Writing directly for the parents involved, Julian Sleigh shows the young person awakening to make decisions out of his or her own sense of responsibility and feelings. If parents are sufficiently aware of this time of trial and error they will be able to show trust and confidence in the emerging personality.

Crisis Points

Working through personal problems

Julian Sleigh

Everybody goes through a major crisis at some point in their life. As a counsellor Julian Sleigh has distilled these years of experience into a process of twelve steps which help to resolve difficult situations of all kinds. The steps are designed to allow us to face the facts of our lives and to perceive the feelings and emotions that come from within our destiny.

Floris Books

Steiner Education

in theory and practice

Gilbert Childs

This is a clear exposition of Steiner's view of the child as a developing personality based on body, soul and spirit. It describes the child's stages of development and gives a detailed account of the Steiner/Waldorf school curriculum and teaching methods. It will be useful both to those already involved with Steiner/Waldorf schools, and also to anyone who wants to learn more about this well established alternative to the state educational system.

Gilbert Childs worked in Steiner schools for many years and wrote his doctoral thesis on the importance of Steiner's educational principles for modern society. He now works as an educational adviser and examiner.

Education for Special Needs

Principles and practice in Camphill Schools

Henning Hansmann

Curative education aims to treat children with intellectual and sensory handicaps or nervous and emotional disturbances, through predominantly pedagogical means. It draws on insights from psychiatry, paediatrics, psychology, sociology, education and the philosophy of Rudolf Steiner. This book looks at the underlying principles of Steiner's approach to education and at how the educational curriculum of the Waldorf schools is adapted for the special needs of the handicapped.

Henning Hansmann was Principal of the Camphill Rudolf Steiner Schools in Aberdeen.

Floris Books

The Beginnings of Christianity

Essene mystery, Gnostic revelation and the Christian vision

Andrew Welburn

The boundaries between early Christian belief, Jewish tradition and the ancient pagan mysteries start to fade in the light of modern archaeological finds at Qumran and Nag Hammadi and of Rudolf Steiner's spiritual investigations. The Gnostic gospels clearly reveal that early Christianity had a powerful esoteric current. This is also reflected in the New Testament writings of Mark, Paul and above all John.

During the early centuries after Christ, Gnostic Christians tried to preserve this tradition, using the archaic mysteries as a way to knowledge *(gnosis)* of higher cosmic truths.

In describing the pre–Christian roots and subsequent development of esoteric Christianity, the author re–examines the canonical texts and the perplexing figures of Paul and John, both, in their own way, initiates into higher awareness.

The Gnostic sects were finally suppressed by an orthodoxy which had lost sight of "the dynamic of the self," the author concludes. He discovers a real kinship between our own age and the early Christians, and shows how, in a way not possible for the Reformation Church, we now have the chance to rediscover the spiritual world and meaning of Christian beginnings.

Floris Books